# Train Your Team Yourself

# Train Your Team Yourself

*How to design and deliver effective in-house training courses*

**LISA HADFIELD-LAW**

**How To Books**

Published by How To Books Ltd,
3 Newtec Place, Magdalen Road,
Oxford OX4 1RE, United Kingdom.
Tel: (01865) 793806. Fax: (01865) 248780.
e-mail: info@howtobooks.co.uk
www.howtobooks.co.uk

British Library Cataloguing in Publication Data
A catalogue record for this book is available from
the British Library

Cover design by Baseline Arts Ltd, Oxford
Cartoons by Mike Flanagan

Produced for How To Books by Deer Park Productions
Typeset by PDQ Typesetting, Newcastle-under-Lyme, Staffs
Printed and bound by Bell & Bain, Glasgow

NOTE: The material contained in this book is set out in good
faith for general guidance and no liability can be accepted
for loss or expense incurred as a result of relying in particular
circumstances on statements made in the book. Laws and
regulations are complex and liable to change, and readers should
check the current position with the relevant authorities before
making personal arrangements.

# Contents

# Preface

Like many organisations, both large and small, yours may well be frittering away large quantities of your budget and profit. Few would argue that investing in your team is essential, and one of the most fruitful ways you can invest is by training employees properly. Yet, so many of us funnel thousands of pounds each year into sophisticated recruitment and selection processes, only to scupper our chances of success by leaving our new employees to find out how to do their job, by just getting on with it. At best, this results in team members who take longer to settle into their role, in unnecessary anxiety and sub-optimal performance.

Many teams send their members on expensive courses, incurring additional travel expenses and accommodation costs. In an attempt to meet the needs of all the course participants, the aims and objectives of such training are often vague and generalised. Repeatedly, the only people who benefit are those who run such courses.

The answer to this problem is much closer than many team leaders will admit. When asked why they don't arrange training for their own teams, the response is, almost always, that they don't have time. It may be worth considering the savings to be made by training your own team members:

1. You know exactly what you want your team members to do.
2. You know exactly what preparation they need.
3. You or other members of your team have the knowledge and the skills to provide the right preparation.

Perhaps the real reason why you have not spent more time training your own team members is that you do not think you have the tools to provide such training. If you have the knowledge and skills to lead your team, and good interpersonal skills, you are most of the way towards training your own team. Some of you will want to provide technical training in IT skills. Others will want to arm your team members with some of the 'softer skills' such as handling difficult clients or working together as a team. Whatever training you want to provide yourself, within your own team, is very probably within your reach. There are a few principles of learning you will need to be aware of; strategies for setting up training sessions; different ways of delivering training and how to elicit feedback. Before you do any of this, though, you will need to identify what your team **need** to learn about, not what you want to train them to do. There is a difference.

*Lisa Hadfield-Law*

---

**A good teacher is one whose spirit enters the soul of the pupil**
*John Milton*

# 1

## Principles of Teaching and Learning

> **'The mind is not a vessel to be filled, but a fire to be ignited'**
> *Plutarch*

### WHAT IS LEARNING?

Learning can be described as a relatively permanent change in behaviour, which comes about as the result of a planned experience.

There are three areas of change you will need to consider when planning and delivering training:

- knowledge
- skills
- attitude.

The old idea of learning was rooted in the concept of the mind being a blank sheet, waiting to have knowledge 'written on it'. The job of the teacher was to provide a steady flow of information and wisdom to fill the space. The educated person would then be able to refer mentally to this encyclopaedia of knowledge, in order to deal with day to day problems. There is still a tendency for us to think that if we *tell* somebody something, then they will know it. It is easy to forget that knowledge is useless unless it makes a difference to what you do or gives you more choices.

Teachers now know that learning can and must encompass far more than just facts. It is not a spectator sport. It includes acquiring an awareness of ideas, values, skills and principles. As a result of this, **attitude** is now acknowledged to be the most important aspect of teaching, but is still the least planned for. A great deal of attention is paid to knowledge and skills, which are easier to address, but attitude has been neglected. Before you even start to consider training requirements, you must decide what you *want* to change. Put simply, what do you want your trainees to be able to do, know, feel or be, that is different to what they can do, what they know, what they feel, or what they are, now?

## HOW DO YOU INFLUENCE ATTITUDE?

Given that attitude is so important when considering training, you can influence your team members in a number of ways:

1.  If you have standards or policies in place, pertaining to the area in which you are training, make sure you adhere strictly to them. You will need to stick to them both during training and in practice. This can be a nuisance at times, particularly when you want to cut corners and save time, but to sacrifice standards you have set will cast doubt on your credibility and the credibility of everything else you have taught your team members. If you were guiding a police officer through the process of making an arrest, you would adhere strictly to the procedure laid down, both during training and in real life. Should you compromise, confusion and difficulties

would be bound to arise eventually. The repercussions could be very serious and the resultant difficulties costly, in terms of time and money.

2. For most of our teams, interpersonal skills are essential. The way we handle team members during training will affect the way they treat others. You set the tone for the way they deal with people. If you treat trainees with sensitivity and respect, you will find that they will take the lead from you and deal with others sensitively and respectfully, be they colleagues, suppliers or customers. Similarly, if you behave in an arrogant and inconsiderate way, you will see your behaviour mirrored in their dealings with others.

3. Role modelling is one of the most powerful ways you can shape your team. You will find that behaving at work the way you want to see your team members behave has more influence than anything you tell them to do or be. If the senior partner in a firm of accountants gets her bills out to clients by the 1st of every month, she is much more likely to ensure that the rest of the staff do the same, than if she sends an email round to each member of the team, telling them to do so. Actions speak louder than words.

People learn most from how others are, rather than what they say. You, as a team leader, must not just accept, but delight in being a continuous learner. If you want your team to embrace progress and development, they must see you embracing the same. During training you can:

- have fun
- show it is acceptable to experiment
- admit you are not sure something will work
- actively seek opportunities to learn
- take risks rather than play safe
- shift from being the expert to helping the team learn.

## WHAT IS TRAINING?

> **Training can be described as a planned experience,**
> **which brings about a change in behaviour**

As a team leader, you are responsible for:

- identifying the desired change in the behaviour of your team members
- outlining options for helping them make the change
- organising training content and resources
- setting up a suitable learning environment
- delivering training yourself
- evaluating whether the desired change has taken place.

The ultimate aim is to get your team members to *want* to learn what you think they need to learn.

## THE WAM FACTOR

Identifying the WAM (What About Me) factor is crucial to the success of your training. If you are able to identify what drives individual team members, you can use it to motivate them to learn what they need to. Spending time with your team members, formally, during the performance management process, and informally over a cup of coffee, will be a sound investment.

> **'We are interested in others when they are interested in us'**
> *Publius Syrus, 100 BC*

## PRINCIPLES OF ADULT LEARNING

Before any type of training session can be planned, principles of adult learning should be considered carefully. The following seven principles will provide a useful starting point for you.

1.  Learning depends on **motivation**
    *   this is the key and the most powerful factor
    *   remember, get them to *want* what they need.

2.  The training experience must be **meaningful** to team members
    *   useful
    *   relevant to problems encountered/perceived
    *   interesting
    *   pitched at the right level.

3.  The trainee should be **actively involved**
    *   it will make learning much quicker and more permanent
    *   is even more important for adults than children
    *   passive and dependent trainees will lose interest
    *   just as with leadership, the more power and control passed to team members will result in more influence for the trainer
    *   motion increases the intensity of their emotion.

4.  Clear **goals** must be set
    *   if you don't know where you're going, any road will take you there.

5.  **Feedback** must be provided
    *   regularly and in a timely way
    *   with a balanced approach.

6.  Trainees must have the **capacity** to learn
    *   if they are feeling overstretched, they will find it difficult to learn
    *   overtired trainees find it difficult to retain content.

7.  Regular **review** is essential for high recall rates
    *   within one day, trainees will remember only about 20% of the previous day's input.

## STRUCTURING THE LEARNING EXPERIENCE

Every planned training episode should have three elements:

1. **Introduction**
2. **Body**
3. **Conclusion**.

Trainers will often neglect the introduction and conclusion of a session in favour of fitting in as much material as possible. However, these two parts are probably more important than the body. Some consider that if you get your introduction and conclusion right, if time is short, most of the body of the training can be postponed. Usually trainers will rush straight into the main body without any introduction and then peter out at the end with a 'Well that's about it, I think.'

---

**If you fail to prepare, you are preparing to fail**

---

**1. Introduction**
The introduction could be considered to be the most important part of any training session. It is at this point that concentration is at its highest. The following issues will need to be carefully considered before the main part of the session is started:

**R** *Establish Roles* Your job and the trainees' job
  • what you're going to do
  • what you want from them.

**O** *Objectives* If you don't know where you're going, any road will do
  • don't just list wordy outcomes
  • identify problems or questions.

**L** *Link or Overview* Importance of the session and your pegs on which to hang information.

**E** *Environment* Preparing a suitable learning environment can make the difference between success and failure. How to prepare the environment for different types of delivery will be covered later in the book.

## 2. Body

This is the main part of the training session.

- This section is the most familiar to most people and is often the only bit of the session delivered.

- Giving control over to trainees for what they learn is a risk, but is usually worth it.

- Even though there might be only one person talking, it doesn't need to be strictly monologue, as long as there is dialogue between minds. Remember, the active learner learns.

- Chunk into 10–15 minute sections. People are able to concentrate for only about 8–13 minutes at once. If you pause every 10–15 minutes or change the mode of delivery, trainees will be able to retain much more.

## 3. Conclusion

Once it is clear that you are approaching the end of the session, your trainees' concentration will be high again, so it is worth taking advantage of this. The last few minutes must be protected time to answer any questions and take the final opportunity to drive home the most important messages from your training.

- **Keep to time**. If trainees realise you are running over time, they will tend to stop listening and start to think about what they should be or will be doing next. Don't ever run over time, just cut the body and make sure your introduction and conclusion are gold standard. If you rehearse a session, remember that you are likely to take 25–50% longer on the day. Early finishes, by a few minutes, are fine. Late ones are not.

- **Revisiting objectives** is a good way of both making sure you have covered what you were supposed to and also of reinforcing the most important points.

- You will need to leave a few minutes for **questions**. If there is not enough time to cover all the questions in the group, you must make yourself available to answer any outstanding ones afterwards. Questions should be dealt with **before** the conclusion, so that trainees hear what **you** want them to hear, last.

- **Warn the trainees** that you are summarising. They will then know that they will need to concentrate hard at this juncture – for example:
  - 'Let's go over the main points'
  - 'Sandy, will you summarise?'

- Finally the session needs to be **finished** properly, it should not just peter out. You can do this in a number of ways, e.g. breaking eye contact or saying 'Time to go for coffee ...'

## SUMMARY

1. Learning can be described as a relatively permanent change in behaviour, which comes about as the result of a planned experience.

2. There are three areas of change you will need to consider when planning and delivering training:
   - Knowledge
   - Skills
   - Attitude.

3. Attitude is the most important area of change but is rarely planned for.

4. Take time to identify the WAM factor – What About Me?

5. Consider the seven principles of adult learning:
   - Motivation
   - Meaningful
   - Active involvement
   - Goal driven
   - Feedback
   - Capacity to learn
   - Review.

6. Every planned training episode should have three
   elements:
   - Introduction
   - Body
   - Conclusion.

Once the principles of teaching and learning have been
considered, you can start to plan the best way of delivering
your training.

## ACTION POINTS

1. Are you able to identify the WAM factor for each of
   your team members?
   - If so, can you write each one in a sentence?
   - If not, how do you plan to find out?

2. Think about your team. What methods of influencing
   their attitudes would be most appropriate for them?

3. Reflect on a training session you have set up over the last
   six months. How did you tackle the three elements of
   introduction, body and conclusion? How would you
   approach the session differently using these three
   elements properly?

4. Consider a session you would like to set up in the next
   six months.

   a. What change in behaviour do you want to achieve?
   - Knowledge
   - Skills
   - Attitude.

   b. What measures will you take to underpin it with the
   seven principles of adult learning?

# 2

# What Training Does your Team Need?

## TRAINING NEEDS ANALYSIS

One of the cardinal mistakes team leaders make, is to set up training for their teams before considering what they really need. A training need occurs where there is a gap between what you require of a team member in their role and what they are able to deliver. A training needs analysis determines if a gap in knowledge, skills or attitudes exists and what would fill that gap appropriately.

## IDENTIFYING THE GAP

It may be that a change in practice in your area has precipitated a training requirement. A piece of new equipment or legislation may have training implications. However, a gap may not always be so obvious. You may pick up hints from:

- complaints from team members, suppliers or clients
- repeated mistakes
- accident reports
- conflict within the team
- missed performance targets
- high staff turnover
- exit interviews
- absenteeism.

Once you have identified a gap, you will need to start to fill it immediately and appropriately. You will need to gather information including:

- job descriptions for each member
- person specifications for each member
- team and individual objectives
- the team mission statement.

If this information is not available, then you may need to start exploring your own training needs for successful recruitment and selection, performance management and team leadership.

## IS TRAINING THE BEST OPTION?

Training is a tempting option for team leaders in some situations. It is reasonably simple to set up and make sure all your team have taken part, in the hope that it will protect you, in some way, from the criticism of employees, employers or clients. Training is not always the most appropriate option, though. There may be better ways of filling gaps. You may need to ask yourself some fundamental questions such as:

- Is this team member in the correct role?
- Should our team be involved in providing this service?
- Am I sufficiently skilled and knowledgeable to do this analysis?
- If I need help, where can I get it?

Before you decide that training will fill the gap identified, ask yourself: 'Could each team member do what is required of them if it were a matter of life or death?' If they could, your problem is probably a management one rather than a training issue.

## BRIDGING THE GAP

Once you've decided that training will fill the gap, you will need to gather some more information.

One useful method for planning training content is to design a questionnaire or hold a team meeting. Those doing the job are often in the best position to identify their training needs and will have good ideas for how to meet them. Bridging the gap between what your team want to learn and what you think they need to know can be difficult, and is usually best achieved following some in-depth discussion to reach an appropriate compromise.

## SETTING OUTCOMES

Once the gap is identified and the broad area of training to fill it has been discussed, outcomes can be set.

- What do you want your team members to be able to do, know, feel or be when they have completed the training?
- These outcomes need to be expressed in terms of what your team will learn.
- How do you want to achieve this outcome?

Outcomes should be:

- expressed positively
- within your control
- measurable, i.e. what will you see or hear from them afterwards.

This will then help you design a session to give your team the appropriate knowledge, skills and attitudes to do their job properly.

## SELECTING A SUITABLE MODE OF DELIVERY

In an effort to make sure that you select a suitable method of training, you will need to ask yourself some key questions:

1. **How much time do you have?**
   The less time you have, the more appropriate it will be to contribute more yourself and interact less with your team.

2. **How much do your team already know about the subject?**
   The more they know, the more you can facilitate the
   process.

3. **What do your team expect?**
   Depending on the culture of your organisation, you may
   want to start by presenting and move towards more
   interactive methods.

4. **How skilled are you as a facilitator?**
   If your facilitation skills are limited, you may be better
   taking a more directive approach until you have had
   time to practise your skills in another forum.

## CHECKING THE TRAINING HAS WORKED

Evaluation is the final step in the training process. What
difference has your training made? Effective evaluation
should be done at four different stages:

### Mid-stream evaluation
Checking from moment to moment how progress is being
made.

- Are you meeting the needs of your team?
- Are they still engaged?
- Have you remained focused on the appropriate subject
  matter?

One very useful way I have done this in the past is to ask my
team to grade themselves on a scale of one to ten, where
one is micro-sleeping and ten is a perfect learning state. If
anyone is dissatisfied with where they are on the scale, you
can look at how to improve the situation.

### Session end evaluation
Where your team evaluate the training and your delivery.
You must also reflect on the session yourself. Evaluation by
your team can be explored with an evaluation form, which

asks for a numerical rate for the training and comments about it.

### Transfer evaluation

Have the new 'behaviours' – i.e. skills, knowledge and attitudes – been transferred to where they are required? Are your team able to put their new training into practice? Knowledge and skills are comparatively easy to assess. You can test knowledge with a written test and ask your team to reproduce skills. Evaluating attitude change is much harder, though. Attitudes are beliefs, values and opinions. They are more sophisticated than skills and are not easily influenced. One good example of attitude training is training to achieve commitment to an equal opportunities policy, within the team.

So how would you measure changes in attitude? These can be identified through careful questions before and after training, e.g:

- What have been the most important things about this training?
- What will you do differently when you get back to work?

### Organisational evaluation

Have the new 'behaviours' contributed to the organisational goals? To be able to assess this, strong organisational goals must be available.

### SUMMARY

Identifying a gap between the knowledge, skills and attitudes needed by your team and those they already have, does not need to be a complex process. However, it can be expensive in terms of time and money, which will need to be considered from the start.

Before planning any training session, ask yourself:

- Is there a gap between what you require of a team member in their role and what they are able to deliver?

- Is training the best option?
- If so, what mode of delivery is most suitable?
- How can you bridge the gap?
- What do you want your team members to be able to do, know, be or feel when they have completed the training?

Team leaders have learned to identify training needs and deliver training well. However, the final step continues to be neglected. All training needs to be evaluated.

- Did it work?
- Were the objectives met?
- Have any problems been rectified?
- What improvements could have been made?
- Has the gap been closed?

## ACTION POINTS

1. Gather together:
   a. Job descriptions and person specifications for each member of your team.
   b. Team objectives for the next year.
   c. Individual performance management objectives.
   d. The organisational/team mission statement.

   If any of these items are missing, start by developing them.

2. Using this information to help you, identify three major learning needs which will be essential to your team's success over the next year. Set aside 60–90 minutes with your team, to discuss a strategy for training for the following year.

3. Once you have decided upon your first training session, write a plan for how you will evaluate its success.

# 3

## Preparing for a Presentation

> **'It usually takes me two weeks to prepare a good impromptu speech'**
> *Mark Twain*

### PREPARATION IS THE KEY TO SUCCESS

A presentation can provide an excellent starting point for any training programme. You can access all your team members at once and provide information, along with some motivation, too. Winston Churchill claimed to prepare for an hour for every minute he spoke in public. It is not just the time spent preparing, but what you do during that time. Faced with the prospect of presenting, many will leave preparation to the last minute and will then rush around gathering every shred of information they think they may need. Such methods are doomed to failure. Few, if any, management skills come down to one magic formula, but with presentations, preparation comes close.

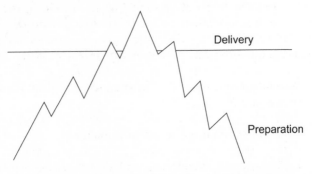

Delivery of a presentation is but the tip of the iceberg

## WHAT GOES WRONG?

- poor planning
- an unclear message
- lifeless delivery
- too much information
- poor organisation
- use of jargon
- lack of objectives
- busy audio-visuals
- inappropriate environment.

Think back to the first chapter. The key to success is associated with three elements. These key elements lend themselves well to giving a presentation:

1. Introduction
2. Body
3. Conclusion.

> **Planning with these three elements in mind
> will guarantee success**

## PRE-PREPARATION

Before you begin to prepare, you will need to ask yourself some questions. Preparation should begin the minute you decide to make a presentation. I try to do a little work on each presentation, every day, until I give it. Answers to the following questions can be written down straight away:

1. Which team members do you want to be present at your presentation?

2. How will you manage to get them there?

3. How many will attend? This will affect how you deliver your presentation, particularly when planning visual aids.

A carousel full of slides is probably not appropriate for a group of three, just as a flipchart probably won't work well with 100.

4. What are the gender and age ranges? If the majority of the team are women in their twenties, they will probably know who Liam Gallagher is. However, they may not know who Gregory Peck is. Groups of men in their forties or fifties may be familiar with Bobby Moore and his achievements, but might not know who Westlife are. This is worth considering when planning examples and illustrations. Your team will appreciate your effort to use meaningful illustrations.

5. Do they have the choice of attending or not? You may need to spend a little more time encouraging participants to listen to what you have to say, if they have been forced to attend.

6. What is the point of the presentation? Do you want to inform, influence or motivate?

7. Would there be a better way of achieving your goal? Could information be provided for reading which might negate the need to have a presentation at all? If not, would some pre-presentation reading be helpful?

8. Are there any current problems or concerns for the group? If you are talking to a group of salespeople who are being downsized in the near future, there may be sensitive issues to prepare for.

9. How much time do you want to take? Bear in mind that taking people away from their roles will have cost implications.

10. Where is the best place to hold the presentation? Can you control costs by holding it somewhere within the building? Is the content important enough to take people off site, so they can relax a little and concentrate?

## PREPARATION

I use the same system to prepare any training session.
However, I find the following framework particularly useful
when getting a presentation ready for my team:

- Identify your bottom line.
- Conceive the conclusion.
- Invent the introduction and title.
- Build a body.
- Pop in pep-me-ups.
- Vitalise visual aids and notes.
- Tailor for the team.
- Rehearse.

### Identify your bottom line
- Why are you making the presentation?
- Why do you want your team members to be there?

Think back to the principles of training outlined in the first
chapter. What do you want your team members to do, be,
feel, or know when they leave your presentation? You need
to express the answer to this question in one sentence, write
it down and make sure it is visible whenever you are working
on the presentation. You will find it helps you to stay
focused on the major issues.

### Conceive the conclusion
The conclusion is the last part of your presentation to be
heard and the part your team are most likely to remember.
Many successful barristers exploit this. They write their final
argument first, and then line up the evidence that best
supports the facts they must prove to the jury. Gladstone,
who was well known for his excellent presentation skills,
wrote down and memorised the exact words of his closing
remarks.

After your presentation, do not be surprised to find that
around 50% of what you tell your team will be forgotten
within 24 hours, and 90% within two weeks. It may be

helpful to ask yourself the following questions:

1. When I finish my presentation I want the team to
   _____.

2. During the presentation I want to appear
   a. _____.
   b. _____.
   c. _____.

3. Two weeks later I want the team to remember
   _____.

As soon as you decide to make a presentation, start a file. A simple document wallet will do. You can then place all the information you need in one accessible place. Although this may not be the approach you would usually take, you will find it much easier to stay focused and achieve your aim.

The conclusion should take about 5–10% of the overall presentation time. You can use it as the opportunity to:

- summarise
- provide closure
- make a good last impression
- motivate your team.

The three to five salient points should be repeated. Most people need you to make a point at least seven times before it is lodged in their memory.

It is important to signal that you are nearing the end of your talk. As soon as the team hear 'In conclusion...' or 'Finally, let me reiterate my main points...' they will listen more carefully.

Be careful you don't:

- Say 'And finally...' more than once.
- Raise new issues during the summary.

- Rush to keep within time. Cut the content, not the introduction or conclusion. These are the most important parts.

- Fail to provide time for questions.

- End on a weak 'Thank you,' 'I think that's all I have to say' or 'I can't think of anything else.'

---

> **'A speech is like a love affair. Any fool can start it,**
> **but to end it requires considerable skill'**
> *Lord Moncrief*

---

## Invent an introduction and title

The title of your presentation can play an important part in the process of arousing interest and getting your team involved. When presenting to our own teams we often fail to bother with a title. The trick is to encapsulate the message you want to deliver, but keep it brief and arouse interest, for example: 'What's In It For Me? – Preparing for Performance Management'. This title makes the content clear, whilst indicating to the audience that there will be benefits for them. 'Explaining the New IPR Forms' encapsulates the message but is not particularly arousing.

As the best ideas seem to spring up at the most unusual moments, I always keep a pen or a Dictaphone close to hand – even in the car and by my bed. My imagination seems to be particularly fertile while driving and during the night. I dislike wasting time and energy trying to hold information in my mind unnecessarily.

The next step is to create your introduction. This is not the time to bore everyone with endless reasons why you have decided to make the presentation, or with a history of the organisation. You can weave these details in, throughout your talk, if you need to.

Unless it is a very formal occasion, you don't need to thank everyone for coming. Start straight away with your opening sentence.

This is your best chance to grab the team's attention. Don't waste it by starting with 'Can everyone hear me?' If they can't, you'll soon know. Even if they know you well, your team will make up their mind about whether to listen to what you have to say within the first two to four minutes. You won't have anywhere near that long if you don't have a reputation as a good presenter. That is why it is so important to start with something memorable or surprising, a short and interesting quote or an amazing statistic.

For example, instead of opening with 'Profits are down this year...' you could try 'Since our last meeting we are likely to have lost at least one long term customer.'

Be careful you DON'T:

- Apologise unnecessarily. As a rule, you won't need to apologise for anything unless you have hurt someone. Don't apologise for the inconvenience, unless it really is grossly inconvenient.

- Start with 'Before I begin...', 'Good morning, everybody' or 'Today I'm going to talk about...' These are tired old beginnings.

- Admit you are not prepared. If you haven't prepared, you shouldn't be speaking. If you really have been caught on the hop, don't admit it, give it your best shot and therefore your best chance of success.

- Immediately harangue members of your team with questions. It is a good idea to involve them as early as possible, but you don't want to alienate them by making them feel threatened.

- Moan about your difficulties, e.g. worries about reaching a deadline or feeling ill or tired. Your team don't want to be burdened with your problems.

- Start with a joke that falls flat. To open with a joke takes real skill and is a risk. Unless you're quite confident that you'll be able to handle the situation if it goes wrong, don't take that risk.

You could try starting with one of the following:

1. A rhetorical question that will engage the team straight away and get them to think. You can control the situation more confidently if you don't ask for a response in words – for example,'In your mind's eye, I want you to imagine you're the team leader. What would your priorities be for next year?' The team can then answer the question in their own minds.

2. A quote that brings your message alive, for example, 'Chance favours the prepared mind' (Louis Pasteur). Sometimes speakers are tempted to use rather lengthy literary quotes, which lose the audience. It is better to use short ones, the relevance of which can be seen quickly.

3. An interesting statistic. If you do decide to use a statistic, make sure it's from a credible source, not a tabloid newspaper. Round off any numbers to make them memorable, for example 'Making a poor presentation for 30 minutes to 200 people will waste over four days', rather than 4.1875 days or 6030 minutes.

4. A story or anecdote. Everyone loves a story about other people, success and personal events, whether they are nine or 90 years old. You can watch your team settle down with their ears pinned back when you start with 'Last Thursday I was driving to work when...' or 'I'd like to tell you about something that happened...'

5. A reference to history, for example, on 14 September 1886 the typewriter ribbon was patented or on 22 May 1947 the first ballistic missile was fired.

6. Dramatic start. A boss from my past once began a presentation on budget management by throwing what appeared to be £50 notes at us.

During the introduction it's important to clearly identify what you are going to be talking about, how you are going to be talking about it – e.g. dialogue with the team or questions at the end etc. – and why it will be of interest to them.

The WAM factor is crucial. What About Me? Every team member needs to be clear about how they will benefit from listening to you. If there seem to be no direct benefits, they will lose interest quickly.

Juries tend to remember only 60% of what they hear. No matter how hard they try to concentrate, the case is not about them. Try to talk to the self-interest of your team at all times. You should then get your message across.

## Build the body

> **'The secret of being a bore is to tell everything'**
> *Voltaire*

From the moment you decided to make this presentation, you will have been collecting information together in your document wallet. By writing each idea on a separate index card, you can arrange them into three to five columns of related ideas. Try various arrangements until you find the most powerful one. Make sure you include only what is important or helpful for the team. Constantly refer to your 'end' (written on a piece of paper before you started to prepare), to maintain focus.

Remember the story of the man on Tower Bridge who was poised, ready to leap to his death in the River Thames. A policeman, a paramedic and a parson were all called to the scene to talk to him. They begged him to consider all the reasons to go on living, but with no success. Suddenly a vagrant appeared behind the man and said, 'You don't want to jump into that freezing and smelly water, it's revolting!' With that, the would-be suicide promptly climbed back over the rail.

This story should remind you to consider the WAM factor (What About Me?) at every step. To get your team to listen to your idea, you must look at it from their angle.

*Remember the Gettysburg Address*
Stick to the KISS principle (Keep It Short and Simple). Use short words and short sentences. You can't go wrong if you aim your presentation at a group of reasonably intelligent 13 year olds. If your team have to struggle to understand any words or concepts, they are likely to give up. When Abraham Lincoln made the Gettysburg Address, he used very few words longer than five letters. Get rid of any clichés and use exciting descriptive words, which paint pictures in the minds of the team. You can never be too clear, so avoid using a long word when a short one will do. It's surprising how many people use the word 'utilise' in place of the word 'use'.

Use pronouns to involve your team, such as 'we', 'us', and especially 'you'. 'You' is reputed to be the most popular word in the English language. Instead of saying 'The benefits are...' you will get a better response from 'This is how your performance will improve...' or 'This is how you will benefit...'

Beware of TLAs (three letter abbreviations). Lots of us are guilty of resorting to our exclusive occupational jargon. Managers are particularly prone to 'management speak'. This can be extremely irritating. More importantly, jargon signals that your presentation covers what you want to say rather than what the team need to hear.

*Exercise*
What do the following abbreviations mean to you?

1. RSC
2. PCP
3. BT

(Answers at the end of the chapter.)

Most people are not able to retain more than seven key points, but even seven is a lot. To play safe, it is often better to cover no more than three to five main points. Once you have decided what you want to say, it is tempting to squash into the session everything you might ever want them to know, in an attempt to avoid waste. However, the minds of the team will not be able to absorb it. If the content does not lead directly or indirectly to the team's 'end', leave it out. Use the minimum number of facts, views and opinions to convey the message. Successful negotiators use fewer reasons per argument, sticking rigorously to the strongest reason, and occasionally reaching for something equally strong to support it.

Some team leaders will claim their presentation has to be an exception to the KISS (Keep It Short and Simple) principle, as their subject is just too complex. If the Bible can cover the whole of creation in 600 words, it is likely that you can cover your area in fewer.

*Chunking*
Certainly the body of your presentation will need to be divided into chunks. The average attention span of a British team member is 13 minutes, and North American spans will often be as short as eight minutes, reflecting the frequency of commercial breaks on television.

Natural and logical linking of ideas or components is essential. Moving smoothly from point to point is an important skill to learn, to keep listeners with you. Transitions might include:

- 'My next point is...'
- 'This leads me to...'
- 'After_____ comes _____'
- 'The fourth idea is...'

When dealing with data, facts and figures, pick the first, largest, newest, latest or smallest. If the team need all the information, make it available in a handout for them afterwards. It is your job to take the team behind the numbers. Tell them what they mean, which ones point to a trend and which ones point nowhere. The secret of presenting numbers is to identify the dead ones, bring the others to life and keep summarising. Don't risk boring them to death.

Lists of three are excellent for retention. If you make use of alliteration too, retention goes up even higher. You can make use of lists of three by using three arguments, answers or examples to make your point: for example, fair, fat and forty, or ABC – airway, breathing and circulation.

Remember to use only up-to-date, credible and reliable sources.

## Pop in pep-me-ups

Throughout your presentation you should throw in pep-me-ups. These can be anecdotes, interesting visuals or bits of humour. There is a tendency among inexperienced team leaders to describe new or complex ideas from their own personal point of view, and to use examples and pictures that are meaningful to them. Go back to those questions you asked before starting to prepare.

- Who will present?
- How old are they?
- What is their background?
- What are their interests and experiences?

It isn't just children who love a good story. Quantities of facts, without any application, can get very tedious. However, gratuitous stories can be destructive to your 'end'. It is essential that any story, no matter how exciting, is tied directly to the point being made.

When you do decide to tell a story, ask yourself the following questions: What did it smell, taste, feel, sound and look like? Keep it short. As one famous speaker said, 'Don't tell me where you bought the matches, just tell me how big the fire was.' Where possible, relate your own experiences, which makes stories more immediate, more credible and easier to remember.

Bear in mind that people are always interested in glorified, refined gossip. Tell your team stories of two people you have known and why one failed and the other succeeded. They will listen and learn.

If you use a direct quote as a pep-me-up, read it from a card or page, so that the team can see you reading it. If you make it clear who you are quoting and where you got it from, you can add authority to your message.

To keep the main body of my presentation structured and focused, I write my three or five main points on separate index cards. I then write the supporting points on another card and place them under the main point cards. I complete this period of preparation by adding a final card outlining pep-me-ups and ideas for visual aids.

> **'Brevity is the best recommendation of any speech'**
> *Cicero*

## Vitalise visual aids

Work at the Wharton Centre for Applied Research at the University of Pennsylvania showed that in meetings where decisions are made, visual aids significantly influence those decisions. However, visual aids should be just that, visible and aids. How many times have you heard a speaker apologise for the clarity of a slide? There is no excuse – **if it isn't clear it shouldn't be shown**.

With the advent of complex computer programmes, some untrained presenters get carried away with the presentation of their slides or overhead transparencies. Sadly, team members will often leave such presentations very impressed with the 'look' of the visual aids, but with no change in their understanding or opinion. Some of us have access to IT experts, and make the mistake of leaving responsibility for our visual aids to them. There are certainly a number of principles to be followed:

- One basic point per visual.
- Restrict the number of words to six across, and lines to six down.

- Legibility, neatness and correct spelling are essential.
- Present figures as diagrams or graphs.
- Familiarise yourself with any equipment.
- Rehearse with visual aids.
- For a speech of 20 minutes, plan no more than eight visual aids.
- Show visual aids only when you are talking about them.

Do not dismiss some of the more easily and cheaply produced visual aids. Use what is appropriate for the venue. Slides for an informal group of five people can be a challenge, as is a flip chart for 500 (see Planning Visual Aids, Chapter 5).

There are, of course, non-mechanical ways of helping your team to visualise your message. If I asked you to explain the difference between a million and a trillion dollars, what would you say? When President Reagan talked about his first budget, he said 'A few weeks ago I called such a figure, a trillion dollars, incomprehensible. I've been trying to think of a way to illustrate how big it really is. The best I could come up with is to say that a stack of $1000 dollar bills in your hand, only four inches high, would make you a millionaire. A trillion dollars would be a stack of $1000 bills, 76 miles high.'

### Tailor for the team

Look for the WAM factor (What About Me?). By identifying what will motivate members of your team to listen to what you have to say, you can focus effectively during the first few moments of your presentation. Listeners need to know what's in it for them.

Speakers occasionally make the mistake of preparing a presentation to be given to a number of different groups, without considering how to change the focus in line with what is required by each unique collection of people. I have heard a presentation given to a group of bankers, and then delivered unchanged to a local chamber of commerce, comprising non-financial people. The presenter was disappointed when the chamber of commerce did not express an interest in providing support for a new venture. Had she considered the WAM factor, she would probably have been more successful.

## Planning the length

Presuming you can decide how long to speak for, the best session is probably around 20 minutes long. Remember that it's better to finish before the end of your time slot, rather than run over time. Once you go over your allocated time, team members start to fidget and wonder whether their whole day will then run late. Frequently running over time is one of the easiest ways to antagonise your team. No matter how tempting, it is arrogant to assume that what you have to say is more important than what anyone else has to do.

Plan your timings on the premise that your performance on the day will take 25–50% longer than any rehearsal. Be prepared to make cuts if your time is short, but don't cut the conclusion or introduction. An easy way to accomplish this is to colour code your presentation into three sections:

1. Must cover.
2. Should cover.
3. Could cover.

Choose a different coloured pen for each section, so you know immediately which section to cut if you need to.

Once you think you've finished writing your presentation, tailor it. The chances are it's too long. I usually have to cut my own presentations in half and take three things out. Then imagine you are with your team, listening to yourself. Remind yourself of who will be listening. Will you cover what they expect to be covered? Make sure you have not included any sexist, ageist or racist comments. These will be sure to alienate someone in the team. Once one person is alienated, others will follow. If you watch carefully, you can see one individual take offence, and shortly afterwards, their body language is mirrored by several others around them. If in doubt, leave it out.

Are there any issues to avoid? If so, why? I remember

talking to a group from Gloucestershire, just after Rosemary West was convicted, who responded to a gentle quip about murder with stony silence. Speakers need to be sensitive to wider issues than those within their own field and conventional politically correct comments.

## Make notes

There are a number of differing views about the use of notes during presentations. I rarely stand up to speak without notes. For me it's like walking a tight-rope without a safety net. Whilst everything is going well, people are fleetingly impressed, but if something goes wrong, it can be very uncomfortable for everyone.

My mind often goes blank whilst giving a presentation, and I can recover my direction by referring to well-prepared notes. These can be used so skilfully that team members remain unaware of them. There are a number of methods including 3″ x 5″ index cards, A4 sheets of paper in plastic sleeves to prevent rustling, notes on revealing cards for transparencies, or transparency frames. There isn't a best way, you need to choose the most comfortable method for you.

Always make a copy of your notes, as they have a frightening habit of disappearing just when you need them. When using notes:

- Keep them at waist level and to one side.

- Make sure they will lie flat.

- Use stiff paper or card written on one side only.

- Remember that pink highlighter is often easier to see than other colours in darker conditions.

- Text should cover only the top two-thirds of any page. If you fill cards or pages right to the bottom, you will find your chin sinks further and further into your chest, which makes eye contact and adequate voice projection almost impossible.

- Times New Roman type is easiest to read, although handwriting may be even clearer. Use upper and lower case, as you pick up words by scanning the ascenders and descenders, i.e. the stalks going above the line and the tails below.

- Block capitals are difficult to read quickly. Without the stalks and tails of lower case letters, it takes longer to recognise letters and words.

- Number the pages, so if they are dropped you can put them back in order. Tying them together with a treasury tag will also protect them from muddle.

- Use only key words, with colour and symbols. The eye can only take in about four words at a time.

- Rehearse with your notes. Much of the memory jogging comes from the shape of the text rather than individual words. If you make a fresh set of notes just before the presentation, they will not be familiar to you.

- Read quotes or statistics from your notes, to make sure they are accurate.

Winston Churchill was renowned for his ability to speak eloquently, and at length, without notes. However, on one memorable occasion, whilst making a crucial speech, his mind went blank and he was unable to recover his composure. From that day he always carried notes with him, although he was never seen to use them. When asked about this habit, he retorted 'I carry fire insurance, but I don't expect my house to burn down.'

*Reading vs writing*
When a presenter reads from a full script, it is almost always frustrating for the audience. We can process at approximately 500 words a minute, whereas we can only speak at around 100. By reading from a script you lose spontaneity and team interaction. Your head will be bowed, making eye contact impossible, voice projection difficult, and

it is easy to lose your place in the notes. Occasionally, reading a script is unavoidable, for example, when reading a press release. On these occasions, make sure you write the script so it sounds natural when read. You will find letters of at least 14 point size, covering only the top two-thirds of the page, easiest to read.

Remember that during oral communication, the communicator generally uses one to two syllable words, simple sentences and pauses at the end of thoughts. Written communication uses two, three and four syllable words, complex sentences and pauses at punctuation marks.

John Hilton, a BBC broadcaster prior to the Second World War, suggested using 'speaking style even when it is necessary to read. To read as if you were talking, you first write as if you were talking. What you have on the paper in front of you must be talk stuff, not book stuff.'

## Rehearse

Most presenters would rehearse a presentation to be given to peers at a conference. However, team leaders often neglect this crucial part of preparation because they feel it unnecessary when it is 'only my team'. Think for a moment about the kind of message that will transmit to your team. There is no alternative to rehearsal. With crucial messages, you need to rehearse until the content of your presentation is second nature. Say it aloud when you're alone, in front of people when you have the opportunity, and take it seriously. Practise as if you were performing, but do not try to learn the script off by heart. The team will see you trying to remember words, through your eye movements. Also, memorising will get in the way of your flow. You will find yourself searching your memory for words rather than concentrating on making your point effectively to the team. You need to focus on communicating ideas, not phraseology. Memorising word for word imprisons your thoughts rather than setting them free.

If you can find people to listen and give you feedback – colleagues, spouse or children – you will always be able to find ways of improving. If you are not able to, you may want to talk to a clock. It has a face and you're able to watch your timing carefully. I practise when I'm in the car. I sometimes make an audiotape of myself, making the presentation, and then play it while driving. This helps me to familiarise myself with the content, so I can concentrate on delivery when I have a rehearsal audience. Lloyd George, when he was a member of a debating society in Wales, often strolled along country lanes, talking and gesturing to the trees and fence posts.

*Making modifications*
If you make an audiotape, or even better, a videotape of yourself, you will be able to hear how your voice really sounds to others. This will cut out distortion through bones and sinuses, which makes the difference between what we hear and what others hear when we talk. Watch or listen to your tape and make a note of things you want to modify. Practise a few more times without taping, but making the modifications you have identified. When you tape yourself again, you should notice improvements. A good rule to follow is to make sure that if you stumble more than once over a word as you rehearse, replace it with another one. One anaesthetist, who speaks internationally, always stumbles over the word 'anaesthetist' when speaking in public. Very few people have noticed that he manages to avoid this word when making presentations.

Rehearsal should take place at the venue, in the clothes you plan to wear, with your visual aids and notes, in real time. There is sometimes a temptation to miss this step and to read your presentation through a few times. This is not enough. Some speakers repeatedly stop part of the way through their presentation and then go back to the beginning. They end up rehearsing the beginning plenty of times, but the ending, not at all. Remember that preparation and practice more than compensate for any lack of talent.

---

**'Repetition is the mother of retention'**

---

Once you have put together your presentation, make sure you have planned ahead with enough time to put it to one side and return to it after a day or so. A fresh mind spots mistakes, confusing areas, and generates new ways of presenting material. This stage has allowed me to polish my performance to a real shine, in the past.

Remember, the greater your knowledge, the more you need structure and rehearsal.

## FROM PREPARATION TO DELIVERY

Once you have put all this hard work into preparing your presentation, don't let anything stand in the way of delivering it. There are only three excuses for not turning up or even being late for a presentation: death, serious illness or critical injury. A cold does not count and neither does a broken bone if it's more than a few days old.

You can plan for other disasters and make sure they are avoided by:

- Carrying a mobile phone. However, always, always remember to switch off mobile phones or pagers before your presentation, or anyone else's. I watched in wonder when one speaker interrupted his presentation to respond to his mobile phone call. What kind of message do you think he gave to those listening? If you are expecting an important call, arrange for someone else to take the message.

- Allowing double the travel time you will need, even if it's just up a couple of floors. You can always use the extra time for familiarising yourself with the room or for rehearsal.

- Making arrangements for someone to cope with any organisational issue whilst you are with your team.

## SUMMARY

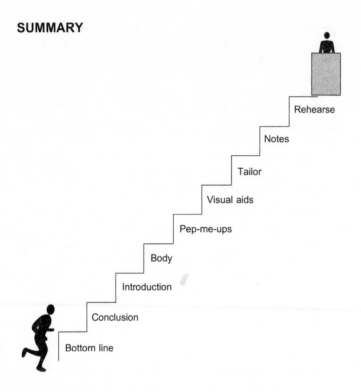

Nine steps to the podium.

### Framework for preparation

1. Identify your bottom line:
   - Why am I here?
   - Why is my team here?
   - Write your purpose in one sentence.

2. Conceive the conclusion:
   At the end what do I want the team to
   - think?
   - say?
   - do?
   - feel?
   Write a memorable one.

3. Invent the introduction and title to:
   - Capture attention/create interest.
   - State agenda.
   - Create safe environment.

4. Build the body:
   - Don't squash everything in.
   - Three to five points and no more than two sub-topics.
   - Do the BAIR test:
     - **B**eneficial
     - **A**dequate – time to cover
     - **I**nteresting
     - **R**elevant to current topic.

5. Pop in pep-me-ups to keep team engaged:
   - Humour
   - Anecdotes
   - Visual aids.

6. Vitalise visual aids:
   - Visible?
   - Aid?

7. Tailor for team:
   - Increase relevance.
   - Consider WAM:
     - background
     - from where?
     - gender and age
     - expectations.

8. Make notes:
   - To keep on line
   - 3″ x 5″ cards – 4 x 4 lines and words
   - A4 and plastic sleeves
   - Must lie flat.

9. Rehearse:
   - To guarantee success
     - in the place
     - time of day
     - in full
     - with visual aids.

So, now you know. Preparation begins before you decide to speak. There's no need to rake together pages of budget statements and performance graphs two weeks before your presentation. As soon as you have decided what you want to cover, start a presentation file and begin your preparation. Nobody would dream of trying to build a house without a plan. Give some structure to your preparation. If you don't like mine, devise your own, but use it every time, whether you have seven minutes or seven month's notice. 'Begin with the end in mind' and then practise, practise, practise.

> **'Practice makes perfect and permanent'**

## ACTION POINTS

1. Reflect on a presentation you have made in the last six months. What did you do to prepare for it? What would you do differently next time?

2. Plan to give a presentation for your team within the next month. How will you approach the preparation?

3. Look back at Chapter 1 and review the seven principles of adult learning. How can these be used to underpin your planned presentation?
   - Motivation.
   - Meaningful.
   - Active involvement.
   - Goal driven.
   - Feedback.
   - Capacity to learn.
   - Review.

Answers to the exercise on page 35.

1. Royal Shakespeare Company/Royal Society of Chemistry.
2. Phencyclidine (Angel dust)/Primary Care Physician/ pneumocystis carinii pneumonia.
3. British Telecom/Bottom time (diving).

# 4

## Delivering a Presentation

Whether you are an experienced or inexperienced team leader, making a presentation to your team will cause at least a flutter of anxiety. Few would deny that speaking in front of others is stressful: some consider speaking in front of your own team to be relatively easy; others consider it to be even more stressful than presenting to clients you may never see again.

Whatever your personal stress level, we know from the Preparation chapter, that the opening is a crucial factor for success. I have found a 'starting ritual' invaluable in these circumstances. I start every presentation the same way, so I focus on the ritual, rather than on my anxiety about what people are thinking. This is the path my starting ritual follows:

### STARTING RITUAL

1. Half an hour before the presentation, I will put myself in the right frame of mind, by having a brisk walk around the building or, occasionally, running up and down stairs. During this exercise I will think back to some of the successes I have had in my professional life. That way I start off in a positive frame of mind.

2. I will make sure I'm confident about the room and the mechanics supporting the session. It sets everyone off on the wrong foot if they arrive in a room for a presentation, only to find the room already in use or coffee cups and waste paper all over the place, as well as the bulb in the OHP gone.

3. For ten minutes or so beforehand I use a popular exercise with sports people, and imagine the session going really well. In my mind's eye I see my team leaving the room, crystal clear about what they're doing and full of energy and enthusiasm.

4. For the final few minutes, I will greet my team as they come in and make sure they sit somewhere they will be able to see and make a contribution. It's tempting to use these last moments to fiddle with visual aids and notes, but it is really important to set the tone for the session by being available for the team.

5. I try hard to start the session on time. Waiting for stragglers to drift in 15 or 20 minutes late wastes a great deal of the team's time. Starting on time gives an important message that makes it clear to those present that you value their time and want to use it wisely.

6. When it is time to start, I stand at the front, place my notes on a table, look at the team, make eye contact with two or three members, smile, pause and then start. I always wait for silence before I start.

The pause before you speak serves three purposes:

1. It gives time for the team to quieten down.
2. It gives you a moment to gather yourself.
3. It signifies a prepared and confident team leader.

## BODY LANGUAGE

The role of body language in communication has increased in profile over the 1990s, although there are differing views about the significance of this non-verbal communication. Albert Mehrabian, professor of psychology at the University of California, has calculated that only about 7% of understanding comes from what is actually said, 38% coming from the tone of voice and 55% from non-verbal cues.

Certainly if you are able to read other people's body language and use your own, you can establish rapport more quickly and effectively with others. Conversely, if you allow your body language to leak messages about some of your inflammatory emotions – e.g. disgust, fear or irritation – difficulties will arise. Body posture is important, as it signals attention and respect to the group. In Western cultures this means leaning the upper body towards the group, showing an engaged body posture.

Recent work in the United States, within sports psychology, indicates that it may be possible to teach athletes to perform better by getting them to use confident body language. Team leaders could use this principle. Confident body language may give you the extra boost you need to influence your team.

Experts claim that the best communicators communicate with their whole being. They are animated and exciting to watch. However, many people are too inhibited to be able to use themselves deliberately as a visual aid.

### Where do you stand?
Stand where you're comfortable. Many team leaders opt to sit down, hoping to look less conspicuous. However, if you are making a presentation it is really important to stand up. It's easier to breathe and to project your voice. But more importantly, you will find you're able to be more influential. Don't be tempted to slouch against furniture in the hope of looking relaxed. It tends to come across as slovenly.

If you prefer to move about, that's all right too, as long as your movements are purposeful. For a long time I struggled to control pointless wandering and rocking whilst speaking. I was aware of this distracting habit following feedback from a colleague, which was confirmed once I watched myself on video. Another trainer helped me to correct this bad habit by making me imagine myself in ski boots, locked to the floor.

Do try to avoid putting your back to a window or a strong light source, as this will tire the team, make eye contact difficult, and offer interesting distractions behind you, not to mention the possibility of your clothes becoming transparent.

Beware of:

- swaying from foot to foot
- rubbing your chin or nose
- jangling jewellery or change in pockets
- fiddling
- messing with pens
- exaggerated and meaningless gestures
- moving around and speaking at the same time.

You can use body language to inject the pep-me-ups mentioned in Chapter 3. To maintain attention, you need to change what you have been doing every so often. Perhaps you can do the opposite. If you have been moving around, stop. If you have been standing in one spot, then start to move around.

## USING YOUR VOICE

Our voices have the power to affect and stimulate emotions, in a way that the written word can't. There is an old saying amongst Members of Parliament that everything depends upon the manner in which one speaks and not upon the matter. Remember that your team will probably have made up their mind about whether to continue to listen to you within the first couple of minutes of your presentation, and, according to Mehrabian, 38% of your message will be conveyed through your tone of voice. Don't waste these first vital minutes by asking 'Can you hear me at the back?' Watch the team's faces instead.

Many dialects have natural modulation where the note in the voice rises and falls. You normally hear your own voice amplified through the bones of your skull, so it sounds different to the voice heard by others. If you do find you have a tendency to be monotonous, it is worth trying the simple media technique of placing stress, inflection or a

change of tone on every fifth word or syllable, to give
rhythm.

### Avoiding pitfalls
Beware of:

- Speech slurry. 'Ums' and 'ers' get in the way. Eventually
  the team will become so distracted, they start to count
  these useless fillers. You can overcome this bad habit,
  through feedback, during rehearsal. A trusted colleague
  or friend can indicate to you when you use speech slurry,
  by raising a hand, beeping or ringing a bell.

- Filler words. Three favourite fillers are 'generally
  speaking', 'actual' and 'basically'. You may have other
  words you slip in when you're not thinking.

- Any bad language or discriminatory remarks.

- Unnecessary repetition. Repetition is the mother of
  retention: when a point is repeated, it suggests to the
  team that it's a crucial one. Make sure that any which
  are repeated are crucial. If you stumble over a word or
  phrase several times during rehearsal, change it, don't
  risk it.

- Dropping your voice at the end of a sentence. This
  becomes too difficult to listen to, and content is lost.

- Slurred or mumbled words, which will eventually irritate
  the team, as they will have to strain to understand you.

- Failing to pause long enough between ideas. Listeners
  need time to reflect on what they have heard.

- Pitching your voice inappropriately.

Periods of silence or prolonged pauses are useful to regain
audience attention. Such silences can be as long as five or six
seconds, without feeling uncomfortable to the team. Pace of
presentation – i.e. how quickly or slowly you speak – makes
a difference as well.

If you tend to scatter speech slurry into your presentations or your diction is not as clear as it could be, work on improving it every day. If you can make improvements in daily interactions, it will carry over into the presentation setting.

Passive sentences are power robbers: 'The customer was approached by me' as opposed to 'I approached the customer.' Two of the most powerful words we have are 'You' and 'I' and we don't use them enough in the context of presentations.

## MAKING EYE CONTACT

By keeping your chin up, you will be able to maintain good eye contact with the team and you will indicate confidence and interest. Eye contact needs to be worked at. Studies show that locking eyes with one person in a group has a positive impact on all those present. Poor eye contact can give the impression of anxiety, incompetence, lack of sincerity, lack of credibility, and it prevents you from eliciting feedback from the team.

It's worth remembering that each of us has a bias towards either right or left when looking at a group and we need to consider that bias when getting eye contact right.

By making eye contact with individuals, when you mention something relevant to their area of expertise, you will acknowledge their input. If you concentrate on those looking bored and cynical, and raise your eyebrows occasionally, you will appear friendly and encourage questions. You will also invite the observer to accept your ideas.

Eye contact is very useful when dealing with someone who might be causing trouble in the team. Once they know you are responding with warm, sincere eye contact and treating any concerns as though they are legitimate ones, gently turn your eye contact to others in the team. Slowly move your eyes away, establishing eye contact with other people as you go, until you are not looking anywhere near the original person. By the time you have finished responding, you're not looking at the difficult person and you won't be giving him/her visual permission to continue causing trouble.

One cardinal rule when making presentations is: Don't talk unless you have eye contact.

DO
- Maintain eye contact for longer than normal conversation: four to five seconds not two to three.

- Remember poor eye contact can lead to:
  - poor rapport
  - impression of anxiety/incompetence
  - implied lack of sincerity
  - reduced credibility
  - loss of feedback.

- Look at individuals – particularly when you mention something relevant to their area of expertise.

- Concentrate on those looking cynical and bored if you can.

- Look at tips of noses if necessary.

- Look at a specific team member, finish your thought, hold eye contact for a moment and then go onto another team member.

DON'T
- Avoid sections of the team.
- Look out of the window.
- Look at one spot.
- Look over the heads of the team.


## USING NOTES

Notes can boost your confidence and help you control the content and delivery of your session. Winston Churchill never used notes until he fell flat during a trade union speech! There are many ways of using notes effectively for your presentation. Try a few different ones out and see what works best for you.

## Options
- No notes – like walking a high wire without a net.
- Visual aids as notes.
- Full script – rarely recommended.
- Prompt cards or sheets.

There are some principles which will help you prepare your notes in a way that is user-friendly.

## Preparing them
- Don't write script.
- Must be readable.
- Use stiff paper/card.
- Pink highlighter is more visible.
- One side only.
- Top two-thirds of the page only.
- Number the pages.
- Should stay flat and in place.
- Don't staple.
- Have spare copy.
- Be familiar with notes.
- Use colour and symbols for emphasis.
- Prepare link words.
- Use short sentences.
- Remember the eye reads four words at a time.
- Capital letters are hard to read quickly.

## Using them
- Don't read from a script.
- Keep at waist level – to one side.
- If you must hold – one hand only.
- Read quotes and statistics.
- Remove each card from pack as used.

## BEING HUMOROUS

> **'Analysing humour is like dissecting a frog.**
> **Few people are interested and the frog dies of it'**
> *E.B. White (author of Charlotte's Web)*

People like laughing. People tend to like people who make them laugh, and if they like you, they will usually listen more carefully to what you say. Using humour in your presentations is not about telling jokes. You don't have to be Michael Barrymore or Dawn French to use humour effectively during presentations. A positive and enthusiastic approach is much more valuable than being able to tell jokes confidently. Amusing real life stories can relieve tension, relax and actually help people learn or remember. There are some pitfalls though, which should be avoided.

Beware of:

- Embarrassing other people.
- Using dialects or telling discriminatory jokes.
- Spoiling a joke by letting the team know you're going to tell one.
- Using an unconnected joke.
- Going overboard on poking fun at yourself.
- Putting all your eggs in one basket by using one long joke or funny story. If you use five one liners rather than one long joke, you have five chances at success.

You may find it helpful to ask yourself the following questions. Would you tell the joke:

- To your mother or grandmother?
- To a religious leader?
- If it were to be broadcast to the whole country?
- To everyone in the coffee room at lunchtime?

Practise by telling your story or joke several times, in the funniest way possible, until you feel comfortable telling it. Try sneaking it into everyday conversations, but don't start with 'Do you think this is funny?'

The most natural expression of humour is a simple smile.
Don't worry about not deliberately incorporating humour.
Most people find something naturally funny to laugh at –
e.g. an upside down slide or an unfortunate noise. Don't
take yourself too seriously and your natural sense of humour
will come through. Even the Talmud teaches that a lesson
taught with humour is a lesson retained.

> **'Laughter is no enemy to learning'**
>
> *Walt Disney*

## GETTING YOUR TIMING RIGHT

Don't look at your watch whilst you're speaking. You may
give the message that you've had enough and want to go.
During the 1992 election campaign, President Bush was
debating with Bill Clinton and Ross Perot, when he took a
long look at his watch. Nobody remembers his verbal
message that day.

Can you see the correct time in the room? If not, put your
watch either on a nearby table or on the inside of your wrist,
so you can take subtle glances at it.

Many team leaders try to avoid presentations after lunch
when people are using all of their energy on digestion, which
draws energy away from the brain. The other more
challenging time is 3–4pm, when the liver is often at its least
efficient. If you can, you may prefer to avoid these times,
unless your presentation involves lots of humour, excitement,
interaction or movement.

## SETTING UP THE ROOM

No matter how informal your presentation is intended to be,
preparation of the environment is crucial. Trying to motivate
your team and give them information becomes almost
impossible if there are frequent interruptions, the room is
unbearably hot and there is nowhere to sit.

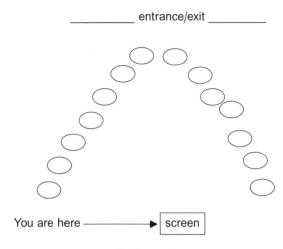

Setting up the room.

Once you've arranged a room, it's often a good idea to double-check it the week and the day before. If you check the room an hour before the presentation is due to take place, you can sort out almost any problem which might arise, from road drilling outside the room to absence of chairs. You will certainly need to check:

- Aids.
- Temperature.
- Lighting.
- Seating.

## Aids
Trust nobody but yourself to check any equipment you might need. Check and double-check it. Make a contingency plan in case it fails at the last minute.

## Temperature
Make sure the temperature of the room is on the cool side. Once there are people in it, a great deal of heat will be generated, and warm atmospheres lead quickly to sleepiness. Find out beforehand how to adjust the temperature.

## Lighting

Natural light is lovely to work in, but windows at work can be a nightmare. Team attention can wander, sun shines in and distracts. If windows are unavoidable, try to make sure the team has its back to them. The general rule for lighting is to keep it bright for maximum excitement. If they do need to be dimmed for a slide presentation, turn it back up as soon as possible.

## Seating

Remove any spare chairs, as 25 people in a room with 50 chairs makes the venue look empty and drains atmosphere. Will everyone be able to see? Sit in different parts of the room and check. Will they be comfortable? Up to 30 people can be seated in a semicircle, and up to 50 in a double semicircle. When seats are placed in rows, team members are unable to make eye contact with each other, which is important to them, so they can see how others are responding.

If you place seats so they are facing you, with their backs to the door, those who are late can slip in. Try to keep a few vacant chairs here so that latecomers will not have to stumble around to find a seat. Use masking tape to cover the metal latches of the doors leading into the room, so that when they close there will be very little sound.

Winston Churchill insisted that the rebuilt House of Commons should not have as many seats as there were MPs in an attempt to make the House feel as full as possible.

It is important to sort out seating arrangements before the team arrive. People tend to resent being moved after they have entered a room and sat down.

The distance between the team and any visual aid screen should be no more than six times the width of the projected image. There must be enough distance between the screen and the first row of chairs, approximately two times the width of the screen. All seating should be within 30 feet of the screen.

When the team have to keep turning their heads to watch you and the slides, they quickly become uncomfortable, and therefore less receptive to your message. Test the seating provided for you by sitting in the outermost seats, with the equipment turned on.

Is the route to the front clear? If you are talking to a small group you shouldn't stand at a higher level. Close any windows overlooking a busy street to avoid distracting noise. Finally, prepare your glass of water in advance. Fill it only half full and put it somewhere sensible.

## RESUSCITATING A FLAGGING TEAM

Len Millbower identifies a golden opportunity for learning, immediately after lunch. As your team's metabolism slows down to absorb recently consumed food, they start to yawn. It looks as though they're falling asleep. Most of us attempt to wake everyone up with vigorous activity. In the process they miss an incredible learning opportunity. Your team's bodies may be displaying tiredness, but their minds are actually in alert mode. The moment is ideal for review through reflection.

Research conducted in the US looked at two groups of students asked to attend a series of lectures. In the first group, each student was instructed to keep their legs uncrossed, arms unfolded and to take a casual relaxed sitting position. At the end of the lecture the retention of each student was tested and their attitude toward the lecturer noted. A second group of students was put through the same process, but these students were told to keep their arms tightly folded across their chests throughout the lecture. Results showed that the group with the folded arms retained 38% less than the unfolded arms group. The second group also had a more critical opinion of the lecture and the lecturer. Perhaps this underlines the importance of comfort when listeners are to retain a message.

The average passive adult's attention span is about 13 minutes in the UK, which seems to be reducing year on year. There is a theory that this is the result of commercial breaks on television. Other evidence shows that people listen intently for only three seconds out of every ten. You need to be searching for feedback from your team constantly, to check they are hearing you.

## How can you tell?

- Look for facial expression indicating interest, impatience, distress, enthusiasm, puzzlement, irritation, boredom or acceptance.

- Watch the angle at which people's bodies are positioned. Leaning forward indicates interest. Leaning backwards can indicate lack of interest or merely tiredness.

- Are their arms or legs crossed or are their hands over their mouths, which may indicate hostility or lack of interest?

- Are they looking around the room for something more interesting?

- Coughing or throat clearing seems to spread as though everyone is waiting for someone else to start.

- Nodding is a very reassuring sign.

If you're still not sure, then ask some questions to see whether the team are alert and understanding you. You have already decided what your 'end' is. Is the team getting there? If you're starting to lose them, go back. Re-emphasise why they need to listen to you. Remind them of the WAM factor. Do something unusual. Change the style of the session or, even better, stop the team drifting off in the first place. Remember that just one word out of place can leave the team behind, puzzling over the meaning. Keep it short and simple (KISS).

> **'The mind can only absorb what the behind can endure'**
> *Mark Twain*

## SUMMARY

Investing the time to prepare your room, so that it's the best it possibly can be, is well worth the effort. Aside from providing the best environment for the team to learn in, they get the message loud and clear that they matter enough for you to prepare for them. Getting up there in front of the team is the most difficult part of making a presentation, for me. However, if I keep the focus on them, rather than on myself, I can concentrate on the job I have to do, rather than on how well I am performing. A starting ritual has been invaluable to help me keep focused and prevent woolliness. Once you can speak in front of other people, you can start to concentrate on finer detail, like reading body language and using eye contact to help you get your message across. There are one or two pitfalls to beware of, such as making tasteless jokes or managing time badly. Otherwise, there is a great deal of scope. You can try different approaches and develop your own style.

The most important part of any presentation is to remain fixed on what you want to achieve by making the presentation and checking you have achieved it afterwards.

## ACTION POINTS

1. Audio tape yourself reading a children's book aloud for ten minutes. Concentrate on projection, diction and pace. Listen to the tape, decide how you want to improve and then repeat the exercise.

2. Put aside ten minutes with a colleague or friend. Plan a presentation on anything about which you feel strongly, to last two minutes. Deliver this presentation with as much passion as you can. Ask for feedback from your colleague, with a particular emphasis on non-verbal delivery.

3. Identify an appropriate area at work in which you could give a presentation to your team. What preparation would be required to get the most from it?

# 5

## Organising Visual Aids

Any team leader who wants to put a message across to their team, without visual aids, must have a simple message and super-skilled delivery. However, for most of us, training is just one part of our job, and acquiring slick presentation skills is not high on the agenda. Good quality visuals can significantly raise the standard of your training session. The vast majority of your team members will be used to the sophistication of television and video and will expect high standards of visual aid anyway. However, you must keep clearly in focus that visual aids should be just that, visible and aids.

Visual aids should be big, bold and brilliant. If your team can't see them clearly, don't use them, as they will distract, not aid. How many times have you heard a presenter apologise for the clarity of a slide, photograph or OHP? There should be no apologies, if it's not clear it shouldn't be shown. One of the major problems we have with visual aids in this century is that sophisticated computer programmes can produce complex multicoloured visuals, at the press of a button. Team leaders frequently get carried away with complicated visuals, but sadly such efforts may well get in the way of your message. Trainees become fascinated by the presentation of the visual aids, and lose the point of your content.

### WHY ARE THEY SO IMPORTANT?

The value of visual material should not be underestimated. People remember:

- 10% of what they read.

- 20% of what they hear.

- 30% of what they see.

- 50–70% of what they see and hear.

- Good visual aids can help make sense of complex ideas. Imagine yourself trying to explain to someone what lightning looks like. Then imagine having a photograph of a streak of lightning available. How much easier it would be to start with the photograph and to use that to build your description. There is truth in the saying that 'A picture paints a thousand words'.

- Good visual aids can break up the body of your presentation. As we identified in Chapter 1, your team members will only be able to concentrate for 8–13 minute spans. Great visuals work well to chunk presentations and maintain their interest.

- Visual aids can be used as your notes. They can be particularly useful for those who wear glasses and find it difficult to look from notes to the trainees. You can use slides or overhead transparencies as *aides mémoires*. If you are going to rely on this system, do make sure you have a back up, in case of mechanical failure.

- Starting with a really good transparency, slide or an exciting prop, helps me control my nervousness more effectively. I often feel uncomfortable at the beginning of a session, with everyone's eyes on me. With just a few moments to acclimatise myself, whilst my team are concentrating on looking at something other than me, I can find enough confidence to begin well.

## WHAT GOES WRONG?

Team leaders tend to make two fundamental mistakes when planning visual aids:

1. They launch into developing visuals which are too busy, too complex and don't work, or

2. They give no thought at all to visual aids and photocopy pages of A4 text onto acetates, which are greeted with sinking hearts by the team.

Don't be seduced into thinking that state of the art support intrinsically improves the session. Never take unfamiliar risks with new technology, progress slowly. Practise, practise, practise.

Visual aids must add value to your presentation. They must reinforce, illustrate or explain. Too many can overpower. There are some basic pitfalls that can be avoided for most forms of visual aid.

### Avoiding pitfalls
*Beware of:*

- Too many words on one visual. Keep It Large and Legible (KILL). If your text were to be mounted on a noticeboard at the side of the road, those going past at 70 miles per hour should be able to get the message.

- Sentences rather than key points. Start each line with an action word and use the minimum of punctuation.

- Numbers presented without diagrams or graphs. These are boring to look at, and team members will not bother to read them, let alone interpret and remember them.

- Unnecessary logos, names and dates. Team leaders will often put their own name or that of their organisation, along with the date, in different places on their visuals. This adds no value and just makes the visual busier, drawing the eye away from the main message.

- Illegibility, untidiness and misspelling. Remember, if you feel the need to apologise for a visual, don't use it.

- Leaving insufficient time to produce visual aids. If you want to have slides made up, audiovisual/IT departments and commercial companies will often need at least five days to produce your work, even if you've made the slides on a computer.

- Photocopied or typed text, which is boring to look at and illegible beyond a few yards.

- Numerous different typefaces. Limit yourself to one or two typefaces and don't overuse italics.

- Leaving insufficient time to practise with visual aids. This becomes obvious when you continually look over your shoulder to check the screen. It leaks a negative message about your preparation for the session, and interferes with eye contact.

- Reading from the screen. Once you turn your back to those listening, they will have difficulty hearing. Keep your shoulders and feet orientated toward the team at all times, and try to maintain eye contact as much of the time as possible.


## USING COLOUR AND FONTS

Colour, either too much or too little, is often a problem. Be careful about using red and green for text, as some of your team may be colour blind.

- The initial attention span per visual aid averages eight seconds.

- This increases to eleven seconds as colour is added.

- Photo backgrounds increase attention span initially to 16 seconds.

- Two or three colours are enough, except when using photographs or video.

- Men prefer and remember violet, dark blue, olive green and yellow.

- Women recall best with dark blue, followed by olive green, yellow and red.

- Blue seems to be the favourite colour of most people.

**When choosing fonts for text, choose Helvetica, Arial or another sans serif bold print**, which is easier to read on a screen, particularly from a distance or if the equipment is slightly out of focus. Sans serif does not have the little feet which connect letters the way serif does. The connections make it easier to read books or newsprint, but not words on a screen. Choose 26–30 point size for maximum visibility.

## USING CHARTS AND GRAPHS

Good graphics give the viewer the greatest number of ideas in the shortest time, with the least ink, in the smallest space. Limit the data you present to the essential. Too much will overface your team and they will lose interest quickly. If you are using pie charts:

- Make sure your 'slices of pie' accurately represent the figures.

- Make sure all numbers and calculations are correct.

When your team pick up inconsistencies, they tend to focus on them and lose the thread of the presentation. You will also lose credibility. If the data is inaccurate, what about the rest of the information? Some team leaders use three-dimensional bar charts, which might look more exciting, but are more difficult to read. There are other ways of making such charts more interesting.

Graphically represented data must speak for itself. If you have to interpret it for your team, it's too complex. Charts and graphs are much more interesting when combined with some exciting graphics.

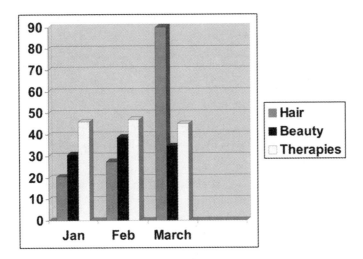

## COMMON FORMS OF VISUAL AID

### Overhead projector transparencies (OHPs)

The last decade has seen an increase in the use of OHPs. In the 1980s it was considered rather amateur to use OHPs as opposed to 35mm slides. However, team leaders are starting to realise how much cheaper, more flexible and more easily produced they are. Overhead projector equipment is also easier to manage and less likely to break down.

When using an OHP you don't need to dim the lights. This makes a great deal of difference when maintaining eye contact and keeping your team alert. The machine can produce a large image and is reasonably portable and available. Very professional looking transparencies can now be produced, particularly if you have access to a colour printer. These can be mounted in frames, on which you can write any notes.

*Beware of:*
- Need for power.
- Occasional breakdown of equipment.
- Noisy fans inside the machine.
- The lens blocking your team's view.

If you have a laser printer and want to print transparencies of your own, you can buy blank acetate sheets from stationery suppliers. Do make sure that you buy the correct type of acetate, as the wrong one can melt inside the printer, resulting in expensive damage.

*Tips for OHPs*
- Produce OHPs without a colour printer by printing black and white slides and then using OHP pens to add some colour.

- Use a horizontal or landscape format, not a mixture. The most natural, pleasing layout is one that has more width than height, i.e. landscape.

- Check for readability by standing ten feet away from the transparency when not projected.

- Use a beaded screen, not just a plain wall, for maximum clarity. The top of the screen should be tilted forward to prevent distortion. The bottom should be at least four inches from the floor.

- Flip a white card over the lamp to avoid having to switch the machine on and off between transparencies. Use the visual aid and then get rid of it. The rule is 'Use it or lose it', so it isn't competing with you for attention.

- Resize pictures on a photocopier, placed on a piece of paper with text and then photocopied onto a transparency.

- Use masking tape to avoid projector glare around the edges of your OHPs.

- Focus the projector by laying a coin or pen on the glass plate. You will then avoid revealing your first visual aid before you're ready.

- Stand to the right of the projector from the team's point of view. They will then be able to look at the visual from left to right, letting their eyes follow on naturally to you when they've finished.

- Look at the machine not the screen, unless you're making a really important point. The use of pointers is controversial: some people find them useful, and others consider them pretentious.

- By placing a piece of card underneath the transparency, you will be able to reveal the contents at your own pace, as well as being able to see what is written.

- Instead of using a telescopic or laser pointer, you can lay a pencil or pen on the transparency to draw your team's attention to particular points.

- Have a system for keeping your used and unused transparencies separate during the presentation, to avoid muddle.

- If you're able to add information to transparencies while they are on the screen, you can add a sense of action. It is also a sign that you are in control.

- If you use water-soluble marking pens, you can wipe the transparency off afterwards. However, permanent pens will not smudge or wear as badly with time.

- Check whether the OHP has two bulbs installed, so that if the first bulb blows, you simply turn the power off, switch to bulb two and then turn the projector on again. If the OHP does not have this facility, it is essential you know how to change a bulb, or how to get hold of someone quickly who can.

- Check the machine well before you start, get a spare bulb and learn how to install it.

**35mm slides**

Although slides have been the standard aid for formal presentations for years, the culture has started to change. In the past, people have used slides ineffectively in a number of ways.

*Beware of:*
- Too many slides. For a 20 minute presentation, you should

use no more than eight slides. Certainly, you shouldn't change them more frequently than every 60–90 seconds.

- Cardboard slide mounts that get warped and jam easily. Glass mounts may cost more, but they are longer lasting and more reliable.

- Busy slides. There should be no more than six words in the title, no more than six lines in total and no more than six words in a line. The point size should be a minimum of 18, styles should not be mixed and the minimum of punctuation used. Do not use all upper or all lower case. Any templates should be simple.

- Too much light in the room. To achieve a clear image, the room must be dark enough. Slides with dark backgrounds and a light typeface work best.

- Use laser pointers judiciously.

*Tips for 35mm slides*
- Carousel slide trays are less likely to stick than straight ones.

- Number the slides to correspond with the carousel slot number, place them correctly in the carousel and tape the lid down. Don't use paper dots to number, as they can cause the slide to jam in the gate. There are eight ways to load a slide into a carousel and only one of them is right.

- Place the projector on a high stand at the back of the room. This will produce the largest possible image and move the projector noise away from you and your team. You can unscrew any light bulbs shining on the screen, to get the clearest possible image.

- If the carousel becomes jammed, make sure the locking ring (the clear top cover) is secure, by twisting it clockwise. Then turn the unit over and line up the two matching symbols on the bottom.

- Always use a hand remote control to operate slides. If there isn't one, it's worth investing in. They can be bought for around £150–£200. If you have trouble differentiating between the forward and backward buttons, put a piece of tape on one of them, so you can distinguish between them by touch. Make sure you know where to aim the remote control to advance the slides.

- Use a blank slide at the end of your presentation to avoid unnecessary glare after your last slide.

- By using a blank slide at intervals throughout your session, your team will move their necks into a new, lower, and more relaxed position to look at you. This will make them more comfortable and therefore more receptive to your message.

- When a slide comes onto the screen, pause for a few seconds until the team has had a chance to focus on it.

## Flip charts

The beauty of the flip chart is the cost and accessibility. It needs no power and can be prepared in advance. It's adaptable, easy to see and available to refer back to during sessions. However, flip chart sheets are expensive to prepare professionally, cumbersome to carry, will not last long and can look dog-eared.

*Beware of:*
- Using writing and colours which are difficult to see.
- Turning your back on your team whilst writing.
- Producing tatty and amateur looking visuals.
- Using flip charts with teams who have been overexposed to them during other training.

*Tips for flip charts*
- Stay on the right side (the team's) of the easel, and point with the right hand, to avoid getting in the way.

- Make sure you have enough clean sheets of paper.

- Have appropriate flip chart pens. Water-soluble markers, as opposed to permanent markers, do not mark the pages underneath. You will often find dry white board pens placed mistakenly next to flip charts. These work properly for only a few words, before they appear to run out.

- Letters need to be at least one inch tall for each 15' to the back row of people. Thick letters in lower case, made with the fat side of the pen, are more easily read. Graph paper helps consistency.

- Black or blue ink is clearest for text.

- Restrict text to the top two-thirds and the right two-thirds of the sheet, for visibility.

- Mistakes can be rectified with correction fluid.

- Bulldog clips will hold used pages over the back of the easel.

- Pre-scored pages can be torn off neatly.

- For fast access to pages, tear off the corner of the previous one or place Post Its® on the edge of the page.

- Light pencil notes can be made on the side of the pages, as *aides mémoires* for you.

- By leaving two blank sheets between pages, or stapling pages together, you will avoid marks from the page before.

- A border round your pages can add impact.

### Handouts

Handouts can reassure your team that they matter enough for you to have prepared material to help them after the presentation. They can be used to highlight important points and give details of references.

*Beware of:*
- Handing them out during your session as they will distract from what you are saying.

- Making them so long and user-unfriendly that nobody bothers to read them.

*Tips for handouts*
- Tailor them for your team – don't use a handout you designed a year previously for a different group with different needs.

- Wait until the end of the session to hand them out, to avoid unnecessary distractions.

- However, using the handout as a working document, on which the team can make notes, sometimes works well.

- When developing handouts, ask yourself what the team will want and need to take away.

- Hole punch them, so they can be put straight into a ring binder.

## Three-dimensional objects
Real objects, such as a model or a piece of equipment, can be powerful as aids. Touch is a very effective learning tool, but not during your session. Wait until you've finished before passing anything around. Once team members have something in their hands, they will tune out from what you're saying.

When talking about quality assurance some years ago, we wanted to illustrate the subjectivity of the area, so we gave out chocolate. We then asked team members to pass an opinion as to its quality, judging look, taste, feel etc. We made the point that quality, like beauty, is subjective. The team were actively involved right from the start, and everyone loves to get an unexpected present.

Using unusual or unexpected props can engage your team, add humour and leave a memorable impression. Do make sure that the prop is relevant and will not cause prolonged distraction, though.

## Video

When used appropriately, well-made videotapes can be very powerful and dramatic. You will need a suitably sized television screen, tuned into the right channel, with the tape set at the right place.

| Audience size | Monitor size |
|---|---|
| under 10 | 19 inches |
| 11–25 | 25 inches |
| 26–75 | 4–6 feet |

*Beware of:*
- Incompatible equipment.

- Frequently copied cassettes. Every time a video is copied, it loses 12% resolution, so use an original where possible, not a copy.

- Long clips of video. Anything more than short clips can be boring and will risk losing your team's attention.

*Video tips*
- Check equipment beforehand, which will save time and embarrassment later.

- Preset volumes, by setting them and then sitting at the back of the room to check levels.

- Check quality of the picture in the same way.

- Always cue your videos before using them.

- Always have a spare tape.

## USING POWERPOINT

### Creating slides

Think back to the Preparation chapter. Always plan your presentation **before** you select slides to support it. Many team leaders can't resist forcing an opportunity to use the slides they know and love best. How many slides will the

team be able to cope with in your session? Don't kill them
with bullet points.

### KISS – Keep It Short and Simple

- Choose a simple background, ornate ones will obscure
  your point. Fonts should also be clear and simple –
  certainly no smaller than 28 point size. Make one point
  per slide only.

- Be careful of using colours that clash or are low
  contrast. The projector will dilute what you see on your
  computer screen.

- Consistency through the presentation is important. Keep
  the borders, headings, fonts and bullets the same.

- Take care with graphics. Pictures must support your
  message, not detract from it. When using clipart, avoid
  the tired old pieces everyone uses.

- Animations and transitions should be used sparingly.

- Tables are very difficult to interpret quickly. Instead use
  pie charts, bar charts, line graphs or flow charts.

### Create a master slide

- Open PowerPoint and click on Blank Presentation +
  OK. In the New Slide dialogue box choose Normal Slide
  which you can then use as a template.

- Go to View and then Master Slide. The default
  PowerPoint master slide design template will appear on
  your screen, with five dotted boxes. Keep the formatting
  simple on the Master Slide to allow maximum flexibility
  later.

- If you change your mind about the colour scheme or any
  other element of your presentation, change it on the
  Master Slide, not individual ones. It is much quicker and
  more consistent.

- Avoid using different fonts, stick to a maximum of two
  or three. Arial, Times New Roman and Verdana all work

well and should be used consistently. Sans serif fonts are the easiest to read. Those are the fonts without feet at the top and bottom of letters:

**Serif**              **Sans serif**

Scripted and fun fonts can be very hard to read.

- If you need superscript or subscript – e.g. $H_2O$, – highlight the text to be changed and click on the appropriate option on the font menu.

## Graphics/pictures

- Some of the images are now so familiar to your team that they will switch off from your session as soon as you show a dated image, assuming that your content will be dated, too. The latest version of Microsoft Office has a much larger collection of clipart. Also, Microsoft's Clip Gallery Live has plenty of new free clipart.

- There are lots of ways to import graphics/pictures including:

  *Clipart*    Go to Insert, Picture, Clip Art and click on your choice

  *Picture*    Go to Insert, Picture, Files and click on your choice

  *Web Images* Go to Insert, Picture, File and click on your choice from images on the Web.

- Once you have selected a picture, place the cursor over the picture and right click with your mouse, Select Copy.

## Animation

- These refer to any movement within a slide and the transitions between slides. Whilst they can add interest, focus and emphasis, more often they detract from the message, as they are overused.

- To create animations, click on Slide Show, Custom Animation. In the lower box, click on the Timing tab and then on the object to be animated. Click on Animate and then click the Effects tab and choose an effect.

## Charts and tables

- The chart and table wizards in PowerPoint do work, but they are rather unstable. To ensure security, it is worth exporting charts from Excel and tables from Word.

- **Beware**: Once you have created a chart using the wizard in PowerPoint, double clicking in and out of the chart can cause havoc with your data, for some reason.

## Before a presentation

Check, check and recheck your equipment:

- Is it working and can you cope if it fails?

- Always run your laptop from mains power, and take an extension cord with several sockets.

- Use function keys F4, F5 or F7 to work on your computer screen without the team seeing.

- Buy a cordless mouse or use a colleague so that you are free to move around.

- Make a note of slide transitions in your notes.

- Remove any slide when it's not relevant, by pressing the B key.

- For flexibility, print your presentations out on pages, using the black and white view. To go to a specific slide, you can then put in the slide number and press enter, to go to it.

*Have you got the following?*
- Laptop, mains cable and back up battery.
- Cordless mouse.
- Projector.
- Extension cord with several power sockets.
- Connector cable – projector to laptop.
- Duct tape to tape leads to the floor.
- Your presentation on two disks or CDs, carried in separate places.

- Another laptop in case?
- Access details for a visual aids expert?
- Alternative means of presenting – e.g. overheads or handouts?

---

**Be prepared to continue without visual aids
in case of mechanical failure**

---

### LCD Panels and Projectors

Liquid Crystal Display Projectors are fast replacing slides.
When they are connected to the video port of a computer,
they let you project images onto a blank wall or screen. They
are easy to use, and easy to transport.

LCD panels are designed for use with OHPs. However,
for good quality images, the OHP should produce a standard
measure of light of no less than 400 lumens. The panel is flat
and about the depth of a laptop computer, weighing about
seven pounds.

LCD projectors are self-contained units, which can be
heavier than the panel, although they have everything you
need in one place and produce higher quality images.

Before you demonstrate your proficiency with this
equipment, publicly, make sure you really know what you
are doing.

### SUMMARY

Team leaders often put a great deal of effort into preparing
visual aids, but just as often seem to misjudge their
appropriateness for individual sessions. Rather than
approaching a training session with a structured plan, there
is a tendency to focus on visual aids right from the start. As
a result the session is driven by the visual aids, which defeats
the object of having them in the first place. There are some
general tips to remember:

- Use colour to highlight points rather than to decorate, otherwise it will lose effect.

- Always familiarise yourself with the mechanics of using visual aids.

- Make sure any flexes are out of the way or taped into a safe place.

- Learn how to cope with routine mechanical breakdowns.

- By standing on the right hand side of the screen, your team will be able to read the visual and then let their eyes follow naturally to where you are standing. Make sure you're not obstructing anybody's view.

- Make sure you talk to your team and not to the visuals.

- Once you have finished using an aid, remove it from view. However, leave any visuals up for twice as long as it takes you to read.

There is no substitute for good planning and content. Visual aids should:

1. Be visible.
2. Aid.

Effective use of the equipment boils down to familiarity. It is essential to build your rehearsal around them. You are asking for trouble by waiting until the morning of the presentation to try to assimilate your content with visual and mechanical aids. Remember, you only have a short time to create an impression and encourage your team to listen. If you use this time up by stumbling around, trying to dim the lights or get the OHP working, what kind of impression do you think you will create?

## ACTION POINTS

1. Describe how to get from where you are now,

geographically, to where you would really like to be –
e.g. at home or on a sandy beach. Do it in words first of
all and then draw it. Which is quicker, which is easiest to
remember and which is most effective?

2.  Retrieve some visual aids from a presentation given over
    the last year. Take four, and recall the message you
    wanted to get across with each one. How would you
    change them now, to make them more effective?

3.  Return to the presentation you planned in Chapter 3.
    Now you have prepared the content, plan what visual
    aids would be most effective.

# 6

## Handling Discussion and Meetings

### WHAT IS DISCUSSION?

Discussion is the free exchange of opinion and information that can be open or controlled:

- Open discussion follows team members' priorities.
- Controlled discussion follows the prepared agenda of the leader.

> **'If he is indeed wise, the teacher does not bid you enter the house of his wisdom, but rather leads you to the threshold of your mind'**
>
> *Khalil Gibran*

### DOES IT HELP YOU LEARN?

Through discussion we can organise our thoughts and link with the thoughts of others. It brings learning, enjoyment and decision-making together. Groups produce more ideas. People not only pool their ideas, but there is something about the process that generates more ideas. In an early review of studies of group problem solving, researchers found that production of ideas was 60–90 per cent higher for groups than individuals.

Discussion as a technique is a means of escaping from our own individual perceptions of the world into which we would otherwise be locked. In terms of training teams, it offers the opportunity to question, clarify, explain and defend arguments.

Think back to the principles of teaching and learning in Chapter 1. Attitude is the most important aspect of learning, but is the least planned for. For you as team leaders, lecturing and telling a team what to think are ineffective if you want to form or change attitudes. Involving team members in a well-run discussion can be a powerful way of generating enthusiasm for change, through exploration of and commitment to opinions.

## SO WHY ISN'T IT HAPPENING?

> **'To a man with a message, everything is a lecture'**
> *David Pitts*

One reason why team leaders and members are resistant to using discussion is that they have little or no experience of this method for training. Not only does this inhibit their use of such skills but, more importantly, they have little idea of the correct way of using them in order to get the best out of the session.

Some believe that running a discussion group requires less preparation than giving a presentation. This is not true. In fact, unlike the presenter, the facilitator who leads a discussion group needs to be familiar with the area, not merely in a linear way, but backwards, forwards and from side to side, as there is no guarantee that the discussion will follow a logical, linear or even continuous path. It's easy to get lost if you're not completely *au fait* with the issues under discussion.

All too often, a team will reach the point where someone suggests 'Let's discuss that', which is a signal for rambling, aimless chat, achieving little, but using valuable time. Discussion could be regarded as a process where two or more people exchange information or ideas, in a face-to-face situation, to achieve a goal.

The difference between conversation and discussion is the attitude to evidence and the way in which we react to other people's statements. In normal society, on social occasions, conversation is conducted on the assumption that people accept things at face value, on trust. Discussion relies on academic questioning of evidence and criteria etc. It is a formal rather than an informal activity.

During an effective discussion, team members must be prepared to give reasons for their beliefs and attitudes. They must be encouraged to explore the evidence on which beliefs are based, rather than just saying 'I don't think we need to approach those clients again, once we've given them the information they request.' Discussion will be stilted if people make a series of assertive statements with little to back them up. It will often lead to a succession of unproductive silences. It is important, therefore, to teach your team to proceed from their starting point with logical arguments.

## ADVANTAGES AND DISADVANTAGES OF DISCUSSION

### Advantages
1. Promotes team development and cohesion.
2. Encourages flexibility to modify opinions.
3. One of the most effective ways to change attitude.
4. Recognises individual differences.
5. Encourages team members to discover their own strengths and weaknesses.
6. Participants can compare their personal beliefs and behaviours against others.
7. Cross-fertilisation of ideas.
8. Gives practical experience of team working.
9. Fosters analytical thinking.

### Disadvantages
1. Takes time.
2. Requires skilled facilitation.
3. Success relies on sophisticated listening skills.
4. The team dynamics may affect participation.
5. Attitudes and opinions may harden.

## WHAT HAPPENS DURING DISCUSSION?

When any discussion, either informal or formal, takes place, activity will be happening at three levels:

1.  Structure: which covers the stages a team goes through to deal with a task or problem.
2.  Content: which covers the topic under discussion, the main ingredients of the task or problem the team is trying to resolve.
3.  Process: which covers how team members interact with each other as they work through the task or problem.

Teams or leaders who pay too much attention to any one part of the activity are unlikely to be as successful as those who prepare to maintain a balance between all three.

## PLANNING A DISCUSSION

### Introduction

**R***ole*
- Try to make the team feel at ease. Using first names will help.
- Explain their role and yours.
- Decide and describe how much control you want to keep.
- Clarify any questions before you start.

**O***bjectives*
- Identify the subject clearly and define the scope of the discussion:
  - tasks during discussion
  - what team members will learn.
- Establish any constraints, e.g. time.

**L***inkages*
- Provide any relevant factual information.

**E***nvironment*
- Move to neutral territory and sit in a circle, so each person can see the others.

- Avoid completely informal arrangements like easy chairs or sitting on the floor.
- The position opposite the team leader is the position of greatest power and control.
- Rearrangement of seating after people have sat down, to get the perfect result, can itself create disturbance.

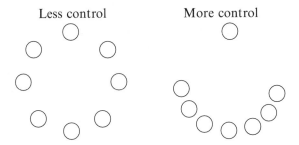

Less control          More control

### Preparation is the key

- Make sure you are up to speed with all relevant information around the topic under discussion.

- Are you the right person to lead the discussion?

- Is it the best way of achieving your objective?

- What do you want to achieve by the end of the discussion?

- How many team members are there?

- Are there too many or too few? Discussions work best in smaller groups. If you get into double figures, you may want to break up into smaller groups and come together to review their findings.

- How are your team members likely to feel about the subject matter and will they be willing to participate?

- Are there likely to be any conflicts?

- What can you do about them?

- Consider some stimulating questions that will get the discussion underway.

- Think about how you can handle possible reactions to sensitive or difficult areas.

- What roles do you want people to play?

- Will you actively participate? If so, what effect will that have on the rest of the team?

## Body

Your job is to get the team going and keep them on line. There are four skills required:

1. Building and maintaining rapport between the leader and team members and between the team members themselves.

2. Active listening and observing of each individual.

3. Masterly questioning to draw out and explore issues with the team.

4. Effectively managing information derived from the discussion.

A good strategy at the start is to make an opportunity, deliberately, for everyone to say something early on, to allay fears of speaking out loud for the first time.

Stimulate the initial discussion, using prepared questions and then let the team continue. Your job is to help them to explore and make decisions about content themselves. This should make sure they recall the main points covered and commit themselves to any action required. The technique has been used since the time of ancient Greeks and can be summed up with the mnemonic KOPSA:

- Keep the discussion on the defined subject.
- Open questions will get team members talking.
- Paraphrase to check your understanding.

- Seek alternative views.
- Argue and point out any opposing point of view not raised.

The style you use is crucial. You shouldn't be dominating, but facilitating, so that the team can reach their own conclusions.

1. Controlled discussion:
   - task centred and controlled closely
   - solves problems
   - needs to be summarised.

2. Open discussion:
   - does not aim for correct answer
   - explores ideas
   - reflects on practice
   - golden silence is essential
   - difficult to ensure all participants participate.

## Conclusion

To reach a useful conclusion, you need to check that:

- The time has been used.

- New issues are not raised if time is nearly up.

- There is enough time for a final summary.

- Summaries are made at intervals throughout the discussion.

- The summary covers all points raised, not just the majority view point. The main points of the discussion should be reviewed, as well as the conclusions that have been reached.

- Key areas are not oversimplified or omitted.

To summarise well, you **must** concentrate throughout. Careful timing is crucial. Make sure everyone knows the discussion is finished. Once you have closed the discussion down, don't let it meander on. End on a positive note.

## BUZZ GROUPS

To get people started it may help to split the team into smaller units and give them a general issue to discuss, such as identifying appropriate team members to assume the key roles.

Alternatively, you could ask each group to produce three statements about a topic worth making. That is, they are clear, succinct and sufficiently controversial to require careful thought.

In order to clarify ambiguous, vague or irrelevant statements, you should ask questions to make sure participants show how their contributions connect with those of others and what their relevance is.

### Team development

Teams go through phases in development. Unless and until the team reaches a certain stage in its development, it is unlikely to perform excellently. It is useful to be aware of the typical sequence in the development of a team according to Tuckman which is:

- Forming – setting ground rules and obtaining commitment from everyone.

- Storming – conflict and arguments occur.

- Norming – there is an approach to consensus and summarising.

- Performing – the group gains insights and produces results.

Although it is natural for the leader to guide the discussion into a neat conclusion, not everyone agrees that this is necessarily a good thing. Some argue that this is false, that it militates against truly open discussion and it has been called pseudo-discussion. It can turn into a situation where, instead of team members being encouraged to think for themselves and follow the logic of their own arguments, they are really engaged in an investigation of *your* thought processes, and are searching for clues in what becomes an endeavour to read *your* mind.

One of the problems of balance, which you will need to solve, is how to keep the group within the bounds of relevance, while at the same time allowing open-ended creativity.

## PROBLEMS ENCOUNTERED WHEN RUNNING DISCUSSIONS

### Conflict

Some conflict in teams is normal and even necessary. Low level tension can be a productive force holding the team together, but sometimes it can break out of control and pull the team apart.

Be alert for signs of the team:

* Expressing impatience with each other.
* Attacking ideas before they are completely expressed.
* Taking sides and refusing to compromise.
* Making comments or suggestions with a great deal of vehemence.
* Attacking one another on a personal level.

The key to successful resolution of conflict within a team is to identify it and face it head on. Understandably, this may take some courage, but in the end the team will fight to progress. The team that fights unites.

### Apathy

In some teams, members don't appear to care enough about the team to get excited about anything. Members may do what they're told but they have little commitment to the team's activity. Apathy can be expressed through low-level participation, dragging conversation, restlessness, hasty decisions, and reluctance to assume any extended responsibility. Almost always, some major re-structuring of the team, some new definition of the task and the conditions for achieving it must be undertaken, to counter apathy.

Sometimes even good discussions run out of steam. If you recognise a dip, react quickly:

- Refocus on the value of discussion.
- Bring people into the discussion who seem to be drifting.
- Engage people who made useful contributions earlier.

### Group think

This term, coined in 1972 by a social psychologist, Irvine Janis, applies to a mode of thinking that people engage in when they are deeply involved in a cohesive team: the members' striving for unanimity overrides their motivation to realistically review alternative courses of action. Janis studied the decision-making groups of selected United States presidents and concluded that there was a common pattern. An illusion of invulnerability and a lack of healthy disagreement led to such major fiascos as Pearl Harbor, the Bay of Pigs invasion and the escalation of the war in Vietnam. Teams sometimes reach a premature closure without considering alternatives, because no one wants to disagree. Leaders can spot groupthink and challenge the team to go further, reconsider and generate better alternatives. One way of avoiding it is to assign one member the role of devil's advocate, to encourage a more healthy balance for the team and to look at things from the opposite point of view.

### Social loafing

Sometimes team members don't do their part or pull their weight. Old experiments with tug-of-war games showed that two do not pull twice as hard as one, and three do not pull three times as hard and so forth. Social psychologists call this social loafing and it usually occurs when it's difficult to distinguish individual contributions. In some teams, you and other group members will need to confront loafing members who don't contribute what they should.

### Interpreting learning

Perhaps the most important aspect of your job is to interpret for the team, at the end of the discussion, what learning has occurred. Usually people have had fun, but they often miss the purpose. Some de-briefing, to drive home the point or get feedback from the team, is usually necessary. Participants may want to continue talking about a group experience long after it is over, and may discover new meaning in the activity days later, but you should not end a group activity without the participants knowing what they learned.

### Unwillingness to speak
Be careful of disrupting thought processes by interrupting. Research findings show that 25% of total effective group discussion time is silence, but it is not common to have more than 30 seconds silence at a time. Team members soon learn that you will intervene with the answers, rather than allow a lengthy silence. This can encourage them to leave all the initiative to you.

### Member/leader dialogues
One of the greatest dangers is to allow a discussion group to degenerate into a series of dialogues between you and individual team members. To avoid this happening, you should not allow yourself to respond to each question, but should either store it for future response or turn it back to the team to answer. When a speaker has finished, you should try to be looking not at them, but at some other part of the group, so as to encourage others to take up the running and not to look as if a response from you is going to be immediately forthcoming. It is also useful to indicate to the next speaker in a non-verbal way, for example, by gesture rather than vocally. This has the effect of keeping you more in the background than if your voice is constantly heard punctuating each contribution.

### Group dynamics
The most effective groups have five to eight members. Fewer than five people limits the resources available to the group. A larger group tends to subdivide, which may result in imbalance. More than 15 participants make it difficult for

people to get involved. If you're working with a larger group and have other potential leaders available, it's often worth actively subdividing.

The group may not have the best mix of skills, knowledge and ability. It may have too many leaders and not enough team workers, or vice versa. Members may not be used to working together. Groups of pilots will usually claim to value team participation highly, but will then sometimes act in isolation and without consideration for fellow team members.

You should be aware of situations where power is used in a negative way in a group, and be ready to intervene immediately. Some individuals may take an informal and light-hearted approach, whereas others may find this irritating. Conflict should not be left to fester. Rivalry between individuals or sub-groups can get in the way of progress.

### Ground rules

If you are unsure about how to set up a small group, the following rules can be applied and may be helpful for all your team:

1. Limit contributions to 30 seconds.
2. Wait three seconds after each contribution.
3. No one contributes until they have accurately reflected on the immediately preceding contribution.
4. No one speaks for a second time until everyone has spoken.
5. You speak in response only to direct questions.
6. The group takes responsibility for summary, direction, time-keeping etc.
7. Time out may be called at any time.

### LISTENING

Before the age of about three we have learned a large vocabulary and grammar, purely by listening. At that age, children can't read and there is nothing to distract them from listening and learning. Communication for the very small child consists largely of listening.

Listening can be likened to catching the words and meanings thrown by others. Catching isn't passive, it's just as much a positive activity as throwing, and it requires as much skill and effort.

It has been estimated that we spend 70–80% of our working lives communicating; of that time we spend:

30% speaking
45% listening
16% reading
19% writing.

We not only learn to listen before we can speak, read or write, but we spend more time in this activity than in any of the others. It is strange then that, although we are taught a great deal about reading and writing and sometimes a little about speaking, we are taught virtually nothing about the skill of listening. This is all the more worrying when we realise that tests have shown that, after a ten minute talk, the average listener has heard, understood, properly evaluated and retained only half of what was said, and half of what is retained will be lost within the next few hours.

The reason little attention is paid to training in listening skills is probably because we assume it is a simple process that can be picked up without training. One way of making sure you're listening is to keep a set of questions in your mind:

- What is this about?
- What are the main arguments being put forward?
- Are the arguments sound?
- What consequences follow?

When listening to your team, it's worth remembering that each of us has a bias towards either left or right in looking at a group, and you may need to correct that bias.

## MASTERLY QUESTIONING

Team leaders often learn to start discussion off well, but then either revert to delivering a mini lecture or clam up completely. Maintenance of a balanced, effective discussion often depends upon your ability to ask the right questions.

### Questions drive communication

Most people talk at about 125 words per minute, but they can think at up to four times that speed. Therefore, during discussion, your team will have a great deal of spare capacity, which can result in mind wandering and lack of concentration.

To keep discussion focused, maintain attention, arouse interest, encourage thinking and explore issues raised, you will need to ask the right questions.

### Consider this scenario

A little boy is standing outside the door of a house. The milkman approaches him and asks:

'Is your mother at home?'
'Yes,' he replies.
The milkman knocks at the door and gets no answer. After several minutes of knocking with no response, he turns to the boy and says 'Hey, I thought you said your mother was at home.'
'She is,' the boy replied, 'but I don't live here.'

---

**If you don't ask the right question, you won't get the right answer**

---

### Why is it so important?

Masterly questioning is heavily dependent on listening. By asking good questions you can:

1. Invite others to be involved.
2. Make the listener feel important and therefore draw them out.

3. Diffuse conflict.
4. Jar groups into paying attention.

## How?

1. Phrasing strongly influences how others perceive your question. Using open as opposed to closed questions will affect the answers you get:
   - How would you plumb in this washing machine? (open)
     Would you use straight or y-piping in this situation? (closed)
   - What do you plan to do for your own personal development? (open)
     Do you want to go on this course? (closed)

2. Prepare questions in advance, particularly the opening ones.

3. Use questions as stepping stones leading to the full picture:
   - Why?
   - What else?
   - What then?

   But avoid 'Guess what I'm thinking.'

4. Start wide, but then funnel.

5. Probe, but avoid interrogation.

6. Where an answer is unclear, rephrase the question.

7. Acknowledge answers positively in an encouraging tone.

8. Explain why you're using questions.

9. Consider the answer before responding. Deliberately pausing creates the right effect.

10. Use silence when appropriate, but don't intimidate.

11. Probe for extra information if more might be available.

12. Check your understanding by summarising and using reflective questions.

13. Use responses to ask another question until you're satisfied that you have the outcome you want or are close enough to it.

14. To get people to open up, ask questions that are listener orientated:
'What would you do to avoid complications?'
not
'What can we do to avoid complications?'

When used well, questions make people curious and even fascinated, which are the two most powerful learning states.

### Avoiding pitfalls

When team leaders start to run discussion groups, they often fall into two traps:

1. Delivering a mini-presentation.
2. Not responding to contributions at all.

When responding to team members by asking masterly questions, you can develop themes, explore issues and help solve problems without taking the session over. Some of these questions and suggestions may help:

1. **Setting the scene**
   a. How do you want to arrange the seating?
   b. What role would you like me, as the team leader, to take?
   c. What do you want to get out of this session?
   d. What do you want the ground rules to be?

## 2. Encouraging participation
   a. What does everyone else think about this issue?
   b. Let's hear from the people who have not spoken so far.
   c. Would someone like to start us off?
   d. What do people think about this?

## 3. Keeping on track
   a. How do you all feel about this in light of the ground rules?
   b. Can someone remind us of the purpose of this discussion?
   c. We seem to have moved away from the topic. How can we get back on line?
   d. I suggest we come back to this later. What about during coffee?
   e. Would someone like to summarise where we have got to?

## 4. Managing time
   a. How much time do you want to spend on this issue?
   b. Your ten minutes is up. I suggest we come back together as a team.
   c. How much extra time do you need?

## 5. Clarifying issues
   a. There seem to be several points of view here, can someone summarise what they are?
   b. We've heard several opinions. I suggest that someone write these down.
   c. Let's hear what other members see as the issues.

## 6. Helping the team reach consensus
   a. Is everyone happy with this solution?
   b. So I take it that everyone agrees with this?
   c. You have listened to the arguments for and against, can someone sum up the pros and cons?

7. **Acknowledging responses in the team**
    a. You look slightly puzzled, Jo. Is there something you'd like to say?
    b. What do you think, Lesley and Harry?
    c. How does the team feel about what has been suggested?

8. **Energy levels**
    a. I get the impression that everyone's feeling a bit tired. Shall we stop, stand up and walk around?
    b. You've all been a bit quiet for a while, is there a reason for this?
    c. It seems that we're all getting a bit bogged down. What do you think might move us forward?

9. **Challenging what's not being said**
    a. Does anyone have anything they would like to say at the moment?
    b. I get the feeling that people are not comfortable with this issue. Can anyone explain why?

10. **Dealing with individual behaviour**
    a. Can we have one discussion?
    b. Let's keep personal criticism out of the group.
    c. Sam, thanks for your input. Can we give other people a chance to make a contribution?

## SUMMARY

Discussion can be described as a tapestry of speech and silences. In order to create this tapestry and to weave the many strands together, you must make sure people have time to think. There must be a relaxed atmosphere in which silence is acceptable and encouraged. Speakers and listeners should be able to maintain eye contact, the seating should be conducive to relaxed body posture and the expectation should always be that speakers have the time and freedom to explore what they want to say.

One of the best ways you can help is by restraining your own natural desire to talk, interrupt or show off. Discussion is not a showcase for your knowledge and skill.

Discussion can play an invaluable part in training your team. It's easy to dismiss it as a great deal of chat with little action. However, planned carefully, you can motivate and influence your team. You can build them into a more cohesive group. You can generate ideas, which can revolutionise the way you work. Finally, it's an excellent way to help your team members retain important information. However, **prior planning and well-developed listening skills are essential** for success.

## ACTION POINTS

1. Think back to a discussion you have had with your team in the past.
   a. How did you set it up?
   b. What conclusions did you draw?
   c. Did you achieve what you wanted to?
   d. How could you have handled it differently?

2. Identify an issue which needs discussion with your team. Make a plan for how you want to set it up.

3. Plan three questions you can use to open the discussion and three more you can use to keep the discussion going.

# 7

## Teaching a Practical Skill

Most jobs within a team have a practical element, which will require some training and preparation. It is often such practical aspects which are most valued by team members. A practical skill is generally made up of psychomotor skills: those requiring physical effort, and cognitive skills: those requiring mental effort. A skill involves a patterned set of actions requiring routine, though not necessarily easy physical or mental activity. Some skills are simple and others complex – e.g. opening a door as opposed to driving a fork lift truck.

In the past, team leaders often put a great deal of preparation into presentations and lectures for their team. However, there was rarely such planning for a practical skills teaching session.

> **A person who has a cat by the tail knows a whole lot more about cats than someone who has just read about them**
> *Mark Twain*

### SHAPING THE SKILL

Let's start with the example of training a dog to sit on command.

1. The trainer must clearly describe the objective as observable behaviour, so that everyone can agree that the dog is doing the job desired.

2. The dog is placed in a specially designed pen and observed to see whether it is already able to sit on command, i.e. seeing what the trainee already knows.

3. Assuming the dog doesn't sit but wags its tail and approaches the trainer, how will the instructor get it to sit? The answer is to break the objective into a series of small steps or tasks, so when the dog makes its first move, which could be simply shifting its weight to the back paws, it is reinforced with food dropped into the pen at just the right moment, through a device controlled by the trainer.

4. Next, the dog sits for a moment. If it's accidental, never mind, more food appears. Then the dog sits for a few seconds. Food drops into the pen again.

The shaping process continues one step after another, until the objective is achieved. This process, where the dog makes connections with the reward, can be adapted to training people and is relatively simple:

1. A clearly observable skill, i.e. an objective is identified and described.

2. A base rate measure of existing skill or present performance level is taken.

3. The skill is chunked into tasks of suitable size and difficulty.

4. Successive approximations of the goal are reinforced, providing incentive and feedback until the skill has been shaped.

## SETTING OBJECTIVES

Objectives must be written as behaviour that can be observed, described and measured. These learning outcomes should be expressed from the trainee's point of view and should identify what the trainee is to be able to do at the end of the teaching session. Note that the emphasis is not on what you do, but on what the trainee is able to do when learning has been completed. This needs to be expressed in specific language. So often, objectives are developed for training which are virtually meaningless and worse than useless.

| *Words open to many interpretations* | *Words open to few interpretations* |
|---|---|
| To know | To write |
| To understand | To recite |
| To appreciate | To identify |
| To grasp the significance of | To solve |
| To enjoy | To construct |
| To believe | To list |
| To have faith in | To compare |
| To fully appreciate | To contrast |
| | To perform |

## Examples

- At the end of the session the locomotive driver must be able to identify what steps to take in response to red lights.

As opposed to

- At the end of the session the locomotive driver in training must be able to appreciate the significance of red lights.

When objectives are used effectively, they link the goals of training with a means of evaluation. An effective dog trainer would never think of expecting a dog to understand sitting on command, but the equivalent often turns up during team training. We wouldn't want to fly in an aeroplane where engineers had not learned to grasp the significance of the door locking system.

## CHUNKING

Chunking is important to break learning into its component parts, so that steps can be identified and, when necessary, learned in sequence. In preparing to teach a practical skill, you will need to:

1. Define the skill as an objective.

2. List all the component parts of the objective: the tasks and the sub-tasks.

3. Arrange the tasks in sequential order and identify the prerequisites.

4. Test the routine for correct order and any omissions.

Shaffer found that typists could achieve the fastest speeds when they could preview about eight characters. It seems that skilled typists can deal with familiar English words much better than a string of nonsense letters. Fluent typing depends on the typist being able to see the whole of an average word, six characters, before beginning to type it. Only then can the full set of finger movements needed to type the word be assembled into a single performance unit. Such a unit can be rattled off at speed. When there's no preview or when the letters don't make up familiar words, such chunking isn't possible, and the job must be done letter by letter.

## MEASURING PRESENT PERFORMANCE

It's usually easy to establish present performance levels simply by asking the trainee to perform the skill. If the trainee can do it perfectly, you can send them away. However, the chances are they will give a less than perfect performance. In some cases they won't be able to do it at all and will need to start from the beginning. But where is the beginning? If the person to be trained can't learn the first step needed to achieve the objective, there may be some prior learning to do. For example, a carpenter will need to know how to hold a drill before they try building stairs. Knowing the performance level helps you to prevent repetition of familiar areas and to avoid beginning at a level that is too high. Establishing present performance level can save time and frustration for everyone.

## DEMONSTRATION

### Real life

The skill needs to be presented correctly at normal speed so the trainee can see the final result and what will be expected of them. This real life demonstration doesn't need to be completely silent, but with the minimum of talk, the trainee can concentrate on the skill itself and will be less likely to lose concentration.

The common sense inclination to demonstrate and describe the activity is supported by research on modelling. The classic studies, reported by Albert Bandura, suggest that trainees who watch a task being performed actually benefit simply from having been able to watch. Of course this doesn't mean a novice watching a member of the SAS will immediately be able to perform perfect landing rolls. However, it does mean that some gains in learning may occur that might not have been acquired otherwise, in the absence of the modelling. Furthermore, it's clear that by watching others who are being reinforced for learning a task, learners are not only more likely to do better with the skill, but are better able to overcome their fearfulness of the task.

### Explained

After the skill has been demonstrated once in real time, you should present it again slowly, so that the trainee can see exactly what is happening. During this stage, the skill should be carefully explained. You should introduce each step and highlight key points with deliberate, and possibly exaggerated, movements. It helps to pause between key points to let them sink in.

## SUPERVISED PRACTICE

Once you have set your objectives, established a baseline, demonstrated what is expected and chunked the skill, ask the trainee to try it. As discussed, this will involve some modelling and explanation, but the essence is action and getting the trainee to practise the task involved. The learner tries the skill and you provide feedback. It's important that trainees perform the skill correctly. It can be extremely difficult to counteract the effects of a skill learned incorrectly.

One excellent way of making sure that correct techniques are established is to ask the trainee to talk through the skill as you do it. If the trainee is quite confident, they can provide instruction one step ahead of you. If the trainee is less certain, you can do the skill one step ahead of the trainee, describing what is being done.

Don't be tempted to take over if things start to go wrong for trainees during this period of practice. It's better to try to help the trainee to continue correctly if you can. It's also important to keep an eye on any other trainees, whose attention may be wandering.

At least 50% of the session time should be available for the trainee to practise the skill. You, as the trainer, should be available throughout to answer any questions or to deal with any problems. If other trainees are involved, they can help each other learn the skill, which will reinforce the value of teamwork. Any newly learned skill, whether technical or non-technical, requires at least 25 repetitions to become a reflex under stress. Even learning how to answer the telephone appropriately requires practice if you've never done it before.

## UNSUPERVISED PRACTICE

If your team member is able to devote six hours to practising a given skill, should they do six solid hours of practice or six separate hours on different days? In general it seems to be better to space the practice over several sessions rather than do it all at once, because:

1. Fatigue and lowering of retention tend to occur as a repetitive task is continued.

2. Bad habits may be formed and further practice strengthens this undesirable behaviour.

3. Frequent rests can allow the fatigue and bad habits to dissipate.

However, there are times when trainees become totally immersed in what they're doing, for many hours, without much noticeable loss of attention.

## GIVING FEEDBACK

Let's go back to the dog learning to sit on command. The dog tries lots of things, but only one or two bring food. Only certain types of effort bring positive consequences. It is at that crucial moment, when a specific action gets linked with a particular consequence, that learning occurs. The process of linking behaviour to consequences is called reinforcement.

Behaviour that precedes a reward is likely to be repeated, hence a reward is often referred to as a positive reinforcer. Punishments, however, are those things that an individual is willing to work hard to avoid. Many of the skills learned by your team will result in an obviously successful result if completed correctly – e.g. converting spreadsheets into graphs.

## BREAKING BAD HABITS

Trainees who have practised a skill in the past, and now want to make changes or corrections, often struggle.

In sports, muscle memory tends to override new learning: the mind has a new and better technique, but the body prefers to do what it has always done. An individual learns about a golf swing that is more appropriate to their body type, but the old techniques and habits actually block the changes necessary to improve their swing.

You need to take time to help your trainees to understand why a different approach may be appropriate. However, after this, practice and feedback will be required.

## CONCLUDING

Conclude the practical skills session by reviewing the main learning points of the session and clarifying any outstanding areas of concern. Allow time for any final questions to be dealt with. It is important to deal with questions before the final conclusions are drawn, to avoid the introduction of any new material. Remember that what people hear last, they tend to remember.

## STRUCTURING PRACTICAL SKILLS LEARNING

As mentioned before, it is often the practical aspects of any job that appeal most to team members. So, you will often find that members are most amenable to learning a practical skill. However, you can't teach them a new skill by telling them about it. Presentations are useful for reinforcing practical skills but not for teaching them. Principles associated with delivery can be linked again with:

- Introduction.
- Body.
- Conclusion.
- **Feedback.**

1. **Introduction**
   - Organise the environment:
     - control outside noise
     - maintain comfortable temperature
     - make sure all equipment works.

   - Prepare trainees and make sure they:
     - can see the equipment
     - can hear
     - know why they need the skill.

2. **Body – five steps**
   - Introduce trainee to task:
     - overview, when and why the skill should be used
     - objectives.

   - Trainer demonstration:
     - real life demonstration
     - normal speed
     - minimal talk.

   - Trainer talk through:
     - explain each stage
     - what will be expected of them
     - pause between key points to let them sink in.

   - Trainee talk through:
     - trainer does and trainee explains steps
     - hesitant trainee – you lead
     - confident trainee – they lead.

   - Practice:
     - don't allow practice of poor technique
     - if they struggle, don't take over.

   ---
   **Repetition is the mother of retention**
   ---

3. **Conclusion**
   - Questions before summary.
   - Summarise key points.

4. **Feedback**
   - Learning depends on it.
   - It motivates.
   - No reinforcement is better than disapproval.

> **I hear – I forget**
> **I see – I remember**
> **I do – I understand**
>
> *Chinese proverb*

## SUMMARY

Teaching your team how to do a practical skill is not just a matter of showing them once and hoping for the best. It needs careful preparation by:

- shaping the skill
- setting objectives
- chunking appropriately
- measuring present performance
- demonstration
- supervised practice
- unsupervised practice
- breaking bad habits where necessary
- providing feedback
- summarising properly.

Resources available to you and your team will need to be considered when approaching training in practical skills. There is no doubt, though, that time you take to prepare team members for their role may well save you time, money and sanity in the future.

### Questions and answers

*I learned the hard way – see one, do one, teach one. I didn't turn out too badly. Are you sure all these complicated steps are really necessary?*

Although many of us learned the same way, we know now

that it isn't a particularly efficient or effective way to learn. Seeing someone perform a skill once is rarely adequate preparation for anyone to carry out a skill. Many expensive mistakes are made and bad habits tend to be formed quickly in the vacuum of correct technique.

*This framework of real life demonstration, trainer talk through, trainee talk through and trainee do will take ages. Surely, there's a short cut.*

It may be that you have to adapt our suggestions to your own situation. However, investment early on in the employment of your team members will pay dividends. It's very tempting to cut corners and get on with the job in hand, but unless your team has the skills they need, they will either procrastinate or make expensive mistakes.

*I think the skills my team has to learn will be too complex to be approached in such a simplistic fashion.*

We have taught teams of surgeons to do sophisticated operations using this technique, just as we have taught small children to tie their shoelaces. We have provided the principles; it is up to you to see how you can adapt them to your team needs.

## ACTION POINTS

1. Consider one of your hobbies and a skill associated with that hobby. Imagine you have been asked to teach this skill to a friend within the next 24 hours. How would you prepare for the teaching session? Make sure you think about:
   - setting objectives
   - chunking
   - introduction
   - body – the five steps
   - conclusion.

2. Now identify a skill commonly used at work that is an essential skill required by all your team members. What strategy would you follow to teach a new team member?

3. Finally choose a new skill that must be taught to your entire team. What additional considerations will be required?

# 8

## Giving and Receiving Feedback

### IMPROVING PERFORMANCE

Imagine you are an experienced pilot flying at night during a storm, but your instruments have failed. You are flying blind. Your radio is out so you can't call the control tower and determine where you are; you can't ask the air traffic controller to tell you your altitude, your direction or the conditions of the runway. The only information you receive is an occasional radio message that says you're doing OK. Are you feeling a bit anxious? We do this to our team members who don't know where they are, how they're doing or whether or not they're producing the right results. They certainly don't know if they are producing the results on time or at the correct level of quality, unless they're told.

One possible shortcoming of training currently available is that there is too much emphasis on the training event and not enough on the transfer of learning. Training is only effective when the knowledge and skills taught are applied on the job. Performance improvement can't occur until team members apply what they learn.

---

**Feedback is the fuel that drives improved performance**

---

Feedback is a term used to describe every kind of information returned or fed back into a system, so that the behaviour or performance of the system is adjusted. It provides our team members with information that they are on the right track, on schedule, meeting goals, or achieving accepted results.

## Why give feedback?

The purpose of giving feedback is to improve performance in the future. How effective it can be may be judged from some research based in the USA. In this experiment a sports psychologist, Bandura, assigned 80 cyclists to one of four different groups:

1. Set performance goals but had no feedback.
2. Received feedback but were not set any goals.
3. Had both feedback and goal setting.
4. The control group had neither.

Results showed that a continuous process of setting goals and receiving feedback outscored the others by almost 3:1. In the world of sport, where coaches are employed on a full time basis, it's taken for granted that the coach will provide regular feedback on performance. It's recognised that feedback reflects behaviour and motivates performance. The same is true in training. No matter how successful your team is, they can always get better.

In work and training settings, feedback is important because past behaviour is the best indicator of future behaviour; unless something happens to alter our perspective, we will not change. Feedback affects performance in many ways. Among these is the degree of pride people take in their work. From feedback we learn, compare what we do to some standard, adjust what we do and learn to do better. It motivates team members by telling them how far they are from a goal and how fast they are progressing towards that goal.

## GIVING FEEDBACK

Often team leaders concentrate on the five per cent of performance that could be improved rather than on good practice, which can leave team members feeling demoralised and demotivated.

> **Encouragement is oxygen for the soul**

One of the difficulties experienced by team members is that their leaders have a habit of saving up feedback until the annual appraisal meeting. A good ground rule if you do give feedback at the end of the year is **no surprises**. A more effective approach is to give continuous feedback throughout the year and supplement the final feedback with a series of short mini-sessions. This will make sure that nothing is missed, will keep the channels of communication open throughout the year and, as a result, the final feedback will be more effective.

Ideally, the more immediate the feedback, the more effective it will be. By giving feedback as soon as possible after an event or during a training session, the better both leader and member will be able to recall the performance and the circumstances, and the more concrete the information will be on which to build.

There may be some exceptions to this:

1. There may not be the opportunity to discuss the feedback privately. Negative feedback in public is counter-productive, leaving the person feeling resentful over losing face in front of other team members.

2. The atmosphere may not be right because feelings are running high. It will be difficult for you both to be objective if either of you is in an emotional state.

3. When a specified period has been agreed and set aside to review performance, keep to that unless there is an immediate threat to life or limb.

## GUIDELINES FOR EFFECTIVE FEEDBACK

Balanced
Objective
Observed
Specific
Time bound

## Balanced

There is something about human nature that makes it easier to find fault with others, and more enjoyable to point out their mistakes, than to praise people's success and to value their achievements. Often team members only remember the negative comments they receive because they somehow block off the positive feedback. It is important, therefore, to offer twice as much positive as negative feedback. Some people go further, emphasising the need for a 'praise sandwich' – two pieces of positive feedback around a suggestion for what could be done differently next time.

Encourage self-appraisal. People are more willing to accept feedback when they have recognised their own strengths and weaknesses. Start by encouraging them to review their own performance and then build on their insights.

## Objective

Emotional outbursts and subjective opinions are unhelpful to the training process. Describe behaviour, not individual personality or attitudes. Focus on what is said or done and avoid your own personal judgements of performance. Concentrate on areas that team members can do something about. It's frustrating to keep being reminded about something over which one has no control:

'It would be much better if you were more heavily built and able to carry equipment on your back when climbing up trees.'

## Observed

There are a number of pitfalls to avoid when giving feedback:

1. Hearsay.
2. Assumptions.
3. Hidden agendas.
4. Previous performance bias.
5. Future expectations.

It is important to focus on the here and now and on the observed performance. Use 'I' statements based on your observations of what happened such as 'I noticed that...' Don't make statements of blame, such as 'You didn't' or 'You should have...' Ask questions, don't make critical judgements, e.g. 'What did you have in mind?', not 'That was stupid, what did you do that for?'

## Specific

Be specific, whether you are giving positive or negative feedback. Detailed information is more likely to reinforce what happened, rather than vague or woolly statements. Be selective. Give as much information as they can use. Too many examples or issues raised will dilute feedback and could lead to complacency or defensiveness.

## Time bound

Make sure the feedback is given as soon after a learning event as possible. The feedback should be relevant to the current learning situation. Be forward-looking. Constructive comments that offer alternatives on what could be done differently in the future are helpful. Discuss it. Don't give the feedback and run. Stay to explore the area in more detail. Have they taken it on board? Do they want to discuss a plan of action? Be responsive to the concerns of your team members. Don't minimise their feelings, as learning can be an emotional experience.

## HOW TO DO IT

Use a simple format:

1. Ask the learner:
   - What went well? (went well)
   - What could be improved? (next time)
2. You then:
   - Bring up any other good points and areas for improvement.
   - Summarise.

I call it the **Went Well/Next Time** framework and I use it whether I am reflecting on how my team has managed the resuscitation of a patient with major injuries or how my secretary has handled a difficult telephone call.

It is helpful for you to establish with individual team members, early on, that:

1. You expect feedback from your team and want to know when you're helping them to do their best and when you're not.
2. When you give feedback, you will expect team members to respond, ask questions and make sure they understand what feedback means.
3. Nobody will give negative feedback of any significance, to anyone, within the hearing of anyone else.
4. You want to know whenever your feedback is not helpful, whatever the reason.

The most helpful feedback defines what has happened and the results of what has happened. Feedback is not useful when it judges the rights and wrongs of performance. One of the problems with using feedback as a means to reinforce behaviour is that people recognise when they are being manipulated and often opt out of the game. An empty 'Well done' or indiscriminate praise can be very harmful to the team leader/member relationship.

### Two-way feedback

Successful feedback is two-way. When you give feedback, either positive or negative, you must give the recipient the opportunity to respond. This is particularly important when giving negative feedback. When people are put on the defensive, they will focus on building a defence and justifying their behaviour, rather than concentrating on listening to the feedback.

By separating positive and negative feedback, we stand a better chance of having our feedback heard. Mixing negatives and positives, we risk recipients focusing on the negative feedback.

Remember that your team members will learn most from how you are rather than what you say. Make sure you ask for feedback from them. It may not be comfortable for you. It is human nature to want to respond in a defensive or dismissive way, but it is essential that you **listen** and respond in a balanced way. Also, remember that people learn best when they are teaching others.

> **'You cannot teach a man anything, you can only help him to find it within himself'**
>
> *Galileo*

## RECEIVING FEEDBACK

Asking for feedback from your team and fellow team leaders is one of the most valuable ways of improving your future performance as a team leader. It also equalises the relationship between you and your team. However, just like giving feedback, receiving it is also a skill. Remember:

a.  Listen to the person who is giving the feedback.

b.  Try to understand their feelings and to accept that what they say is genuine.

c.  You don't need to modify your behaviour. Give the feedback serious consideration and weigh up the consequences of changing and not changing.

d.  Express your own feelings to the giver and communicate your decisions.

e.  Tell the giver what they can do that might help you change.

f.  Thank the giver for their help.

Receiving feedback can feel very uncomfortable, but it can be well worth the effort.

---

**If encouragement is oxygen for the soul, let's not make people wheeze and gasp for it**

---

## SUMMARY

1.  Feedback is the fuel that drives improved performance. This crucial aspect of training is frequently neglected or handled badly. If you look back at occasions you have given members of your team feedback, you will often find that you concentrated on the five per cent of performance that could be improved, rather than on good practice, which can leave your team members feeling demoralised and demotivated.

2.  You should take a structured approach to giving feedback. The **boost** framework can work well:
    **B**alanced
    **O**bjective
    **O**bserved
    **S**pecific
    **T**ime bound.

3. Went well/Next time framework
   - Ask the learner:
     - What went well? (went well)
     - What could be improved? (next time)

   - You then:
     - Bring up any other good points and areas for improvement.
     - Summarise.

4. Just like giving feedback, receiving it is also a skill. Remember to ask for it graciously and use it wisely.

## ACTION POINTS

1. Plan to watch a programme of your choice on the television. During the programme make some notes to provide the director of the programme with some feedback. Use the Went Well/Next time framework.

2. Plan to provide feedback for a member of your team who has recently completed a task or project. Use the BOOST approach and the Went Well/Next time framework.

3. Discuss with your team how you can establish a system for providing feedback amongst all team members, including you.

# 9

## Dealing with Difficult Team Members

### KEEPING YOUR GOAL IN FOCUS

The goal of training your team is to help team members to acquire knowledge, skills and attitudes they can use in the job they do. A difficult team member is one whose attitude or behaviour prevents that person, or others in the team, from meeting their goal.

Your goal is:

1. To make sure your team shares the same vision and commits themselves to it.

2. To minimise any negative impact from individuals on others.

There are usually four types of team member who require training:

1. Participants – receptive to training.

2. Passengers – having time out from work, don't give much but don't cause trouble either.

3. Protesters – want to change the world.

4. Prisoners – forced to attend and feeling angry and trapped.

I will concentrate on difficult team members in the training situation, rather than handling difficult people generally. Remember, though, you know your own team. If an individual could cause problems, try to get them involved in the session early on. At least have a strategy ready for how you intend to handle any difficult situation. Also, try to be aware of any of your behaviour which might antagonise your team.

Counsellors have always had a tradition of unconditional positive regard towards their clients, and it is an appropriate concept for your work, too. Unconditional positive regard means that no matter what the team members' personal attributes, views or behaviours, you will always regard each individual in a positive way, as a person with potential. This can be hard, particularly when you come across 'difficult people'. However, you won't be able to help your team members otherwise.

## HECKLERS

Insulting behaviour aimed at you, during training, is rare. For many team leaders, the prospect of a heckler is a frightening one, but in reality, it's extremely unusual. Occasionally conflict between team members does erupt and will need to be addressed straight away, to prevent lasting damage to the cohesion of your team. The following principles work well:

- Don't take it personally.

- Recognise that their behaviour may have nothing to do with you.

- Separate the person from the problem – ask them in a non-judgemental tone what problem they have.

- If there is no answer, ask them what they would like

from the training that they feel they're not getting. Encourage them to stay.

- Listen and offer to make changes, providing they are within the remit of the session.

- If the behaviour continues and is affecting the progress of the team say something like 'I would have preferred you to stay and work with us but I'm feeling distracted and concerned that it will affect the objectives of the session. I suggest you go and have a coffee. I'll join you afterwards and we'll see what we can resolve.'

- Speak to them afterwards.

- If they return, welcome them back.


## TEACHER'S PETS

This is a much more common scenario, which team members find intensely irritating. This team member will do everything they can to please, and keep offering to help, or tell their personal stories to the team as a way of supporting the training. They can be difficult, precisely because they are well meaning. Sadly, the effect is the opposite from what they intend. They sidetrack and irritate everybody. Remember, though, the occasional short story supports your training and may be interesting and enlightening.

- Know where the short story ends and the novel begins.

- Understand that other team members may feel irritated with the individual and then with you, if you don't control the situation. They may feel that the storyteller is using up their time.

- Acknowledge the storyteller, 'I'm glad to hear you found that approach helpful, I'd like to move on now.' Persistent storytellers should be told 'Your scenarios are really interesting, but due to constraints of time we should discuss them later.'

## KNOW-IT-ALLS

Know-it-alls often feel they know more than you do and should be out at the front in your place. These individuals may also be monopolisers, silent troublemakers or chatterboxes. They need recognition for how much they know. Once you've done that, as early as possible, they can be your staunchest ally. If they are still a problem:

- Ask a slightly difficult question, to slow them down.
- Avoid eye contact for a while.
- Ask them to help one of the more timid team members.

## TROUBLEMAKERS

Troublemakers tend to need acknowledgement of some type, too. They can be extremely useful once they're an ally, but a problem if left unchecked. Often they will seem to challenge issues, not for clarification or to further progress of the team, but just to make their mark. Approach them with:

- Warm eye contact.
- Ask for more information.
- Don't fight fire with fire. Troublemakers can add energy if you use them.
- What are you doing to make them want to cause trouble?

### Silent troublemakers

This type of troublemaker often comes in late, frequently folds their arms and won't make eye contact. They are usually unwilling to contribute at all.

- Try to draw out and reward them.
- Talk to them at break times.
- Involve them in small group activity.
- Search out some common ground.

## MONOPOLISERS

These individuals can be quite disruptive, as they must make a contribution to everything under discussion. The key to managing them is to acknowledge how important they are. Once they are satisfied that everyone realises how valuable they are, they will tend to back off. If they still don't:

- 'Do others have questions?'
- Move focus from them onto another person.
- 'I could talk about this all day – let's get together afterwards.'

## CHATTERBOXES

Chatterboxes can't resist chatting to those in their vicinity. Some don't even attempt to whisper. Sometimes they don't realise how disruptive they are being.

- Pause, then look at the person.
- Move nearer to them, then all eyes will be on them.
- Take a break to raise energy levels.
- Lower your own voice, so everyone has to work a bit harder at hearing.
- 'Good, a question.'

## THE ANXIOUS

The anxious tend to look tense and worried right from the start of the session. They will go to pieces when asked a question.

- Try to get them involved with the planning of the session, if you can.
- Smile, listen and maintain warm eye contact always.
- Avoid negative judgements.

## HANDLING 'GENERATION X' TEAM MEMBERS

One of the interesting challenges with which I have been faced over the last decade has been the generation gap between me and a significant number of my team members. 'Generation Xers' are people born since 1965. The term refers to the fact that they were the 10th generation to come of age in the last century.

Some of the following descriptions of their characteristics may help you to plan training and to avoid some of the difficult situations outlined above.

### 'Generation Xers':

- Are less optimistic about their future than older team members. They expect to encounter problems and worry about whether they have the right skills and attributes to achieve success. They will respond well to being trained how to cope with organisational politics.

- Tend not to feel financially secure. They are always keen to get value for money. You will reap the benefits if you can show them the worth of purchases – e.g. necessary training.

- Hate vagueness. Always expect them to ask questions and be prepared to give detailed explanations.

- Are very protective of their time. Hard work and integrity were emphasised as they grew up. Training should be informative and they should be aware of the time commitment that will be expected.

- Communicate directly and could be considered to be abrupt. They view euphemistic styles as manipulative. 'Could you see your way clear to finishing this by tonight?' when you really mean, 'You must do this' would be a problem. It is best to make your point succinctly with a particular emphasis on the 'why'. It may also be helpful to use their preferred channels of communication when you can, for example, email.

## SUMMARY

The beauty of working with teams is that they vary so much in individual personality. That's what makes them interesting and that's also what can make them so effective. If all of them had the same principles, interests and approaches, the synergy between them would be extremely limited. It is from the differences and the tensions between individuals that creativity flourishes and high performance teams develop.

Learning to understand messages conveyed through body language can be invaluable when dealing with difficult situations. However, don't fall into the trap of newcomers, that interpretation of one particular body language message gives you the meaning of total communication. Just knowing one word in a foreign text doesn't mean you can understand the whole paragraph.

Remember, also, even if you are a trained therapist, it is not your job to change someone's personality or to 'cure' problems. It is your job to help them to function effectively as a member of your team and to help them to get the most out of any training opportunity. At the very least you will need to make sure you minimise any negative effect they might have on the rest of your team.

Keep your eyes open for extremes. You don't need to analyse each member of your team, but you do need to be on the lookout for any behaviours that may get in the way of your team's progress. If you maintain some humility and patience when dealing with someone being difficult during a training session, you may well find that the rest of your team bring the deviant one into line for you. Nevertheless, you must make sure you are prepared to address difficult behaviour as soon as is appropriate. You are in an excellent position to anticipate where and when difficult behaviour may occur. Make sure you consider this before any session and plan how you can avoid or handle it. By leaving it and hoping it will pass or handling it aggressively, you have much to lose. Your credibility and the respect of your team are essential components of effective team leadership.

## ACTION POINTS

1. Spend 15 minutes listing any difficult situations you fear might arise in a training session you are running.

2. Examine each of these situations and decide how you would handle each one.

3. Review the members of your team and imagine how they may respond during a planned training situation. Identify three difficult situations that could arise. Plan a strategy for how you could handle these and then spend 30 minutes with a colleague talking through your strategies.

# 10

## Coping with Questions

A good training event with poor question and answer opportunities will ruin any chance of success; conversely, good questions and answers can save a poor event.

Every question is an indication of interest. You need to be clear about:

- When you want to take them.
- How to prompt.
- How to answer.

Before the session:

- Anticipate the kind of questions you are likely to be asked.
- Identify any problem areas which might arise.
- Foresee team tensions.
- Prepare reserve materials in case there aren't any questions and you have time left.

### THE BEST TIME TO TAKE THEM

- Questions taken randomly throughout the session need a confident team leader to control.

- If questions are delayed until the end, it may frustrate team members or they may forget what they wanted to ask.

- Questions after each section are good to break up lengthy and complex areas.

## THE BEST WAY OF APPROACHING THEM

- Encourage questions with positive words and body language:
  *'What questions do you have?'* not *'Any questions?'*
  *'If it doesn't make sense, then it's my fault.'*
  *'If you're not sure, then at least one other person won't be.'*

- Pose questions precisely if you are asking them.

- Use open questions.

- Listen carefully right to the end of questions asked of you.

- Take your time – respond don't react.

- Don't allow a few questioners to dominate.

- Don't allow mini-lectures.

## THE BEST WAY OF ANSWERING

- Keep responses short.

- Too glib an answer may be mistrusted.

- Try to find some common ground.

- Don't be afraid to say you don't know, but offer to find out.

- Acknowledge the question and questioner.

- Ensure the question is heard and understood by everyone.

- 'Certainly that's something I need to clarify, perhaps I can pick it up in context.'

- Give **short** informative answers linked to some message given before.

- Give the questioner two-thirds of your eye contact.

- Respond with a question sometimes.

- Always be positive.

## NO QUESTIONS

- Ask if anyone would like to comment but don't allow a lecture.

- Say you were asked a question privately.

- Get written questions in advance.

- Ask the team a question.

- Offer to take questions privately.

- 'I expected to be asked. . .'

- 'What do you think about. . . ?'

## TAKING QUESTIONS DURING A SESSION

- It's fine to hold for a moment whilst finishing a point.

- Always come back if you promise to.

- Fine to refuse if irrelevant, but don't do it too much.

## DIFFICULT SITUATIONS

1. *Several questions in one:* Ask what the main question is and answer that.

2. *One which makes incorrect assumption:* Tactfully point out the mistake then answer the question if it's still relevant.

3. *Show-off:* Avoid embarrassing or giving a difficult question: 'That's an interesting point, let's see what the rest of the group think of it.' Be careful, as they may be trying to help, so congratulate them on their knowledge.

4. *Heckler:* Remain calm; look for common ground, but toss negative points out for the team to handle.

5. *Rambler:* At a pause thank them, and then return to restate relevant points.

6. *Arguers:* Minimise differences and draw back to the point being made.

7. *Pig-headed:* Throw points to the group, then tell them you will be glad to discuss the issue later.

8. *Digresser:* Take the blame yourself: 'I must have led you off the subject, remember we are discussing...'

9. *Professional griper:* Keeps making political points. Explain that we cannot change policy here, but we need to see how we can live with the current state.

10. *Whisperers:* Don't embarrass. Address the point to them by name or repeat the last point and ask for comments.

11. *Inarticulate:* 'Let me repeat that' (in better words).

12. *Mistaken:* 'That's one way of looking at it, but how do we reconcile that with...? (correct point).

13. *Silent:* Try asking a provocative question; compliment them when they do say something.

## SUMMARY

You should consider each question to be an opportunity to make sure that your team leaves the training session with the skills, knowledge and attitudes they need. It is easy to leave this part of the training out, or to pay lip service to it. However, if you do so, you leave success to chance.

Anticipate the kinds of questions that may arise. If questions do come up that you can't answer, don't worry.

Find out and get back to those present when you do have the answer. Your team will not only be impressed that you can admit to not knowing something, but they will also get the message that you are taking their questions seriously, when you take the trouble to find out the answer and let them know.

As with many aspects of training, you may be faced with difficult questions or situations, but most of them can be planned for.

> **End on a strong note *not* 'One more question please',**
> **in case it's weak**

# 11

## Team Building

High-powered teams don't just happen, they must be built. The effective introduction of team working has been known to transform organisations entirely. Over the 1990s, the most successful organisations embraced the creation of strong, semi-autonomous working teams. Certainly teams have enormous potential. However, the majority remain as groups of people who work together, but just get on with their job. Simply having people working in the same place is not the same as building a strong and effective team who strive to reach their fullest potential.

### EFFECTIVE TEAMS

The keys to effective teamwork are:

- Delegation.
- Empowerment.
- A strong sense of belonging.

One of the cardinal mistakes made by team leaders, both experienced and inexperienced, is to hang on to control unnecessarily. By maintaining control, the leader prevents the rest of those in the team from making decisions on their own. It can be difficult to accept that those who work for us are usually in the best position to make decisions about their sphere of responsibility.

Reasons behind an individual's lack of willingness to relinquish control often stem from the same problem. Team leaders are concerned about the threat to their own jobs: 'If I give away all my authority, maybe the organisation won't need me any more and they'll get rid of me.' Interestingly, the opposite is almost always true. If the team are able to get on with their work and are able to make decisions associated with that work, you can be available to support, discuss direction and goals, represent your team at higher levels, and get involved with wider-reaching projects and training.

Team leaders have important responsibilities at a much more strategic level and becoming involved in the day to day work will get in the way of that. Psychologists have known for decades that when people are given responsibility, they behave in a more responsible way. Restricting and authoritarian team leaders will find that their team members become resentful and unable to use their initiative. Empowering leaders will help their team to feel valued and motivated.

### Benefits of getting it right
Organisations which have got team work right are finding that people:

- Work more efficiently.
- Suffer from lower levels of stress.
- Make more of a contribution.
- Stay with the organisation longer.
- Take less sick time.
- Try to improve the way they do their work.

### WHAT MAKES A GOOD TEAM?
Effective teams:
- Have common goals and can work together to achieve them.

- Have a clear identity as a special group.

- Are able to interact positively with others in the organisation.

- Generate a positive and enthusiastic approach.

- Communicate clearly and effectively.

- Work together more effectively than each individual would.

## GROUP DYNAMICS AND TEAM ROLES

Teams work best when they are carefully balanced. There is a tendency for team leaders to recruit team members who have similar knowledge, skills and attitudes. Some people call them PLUs or 'People Like Us'. This can work well in a social set up, but can sabotage success in a work team. If all your team members are excellent at collaborating with one another, supporting the ideas of their colleagues and working hard to get things done, but there is nobody who can think up original ideas, the team won't get very far. Similarly, if all members have plenty of ideas, day in and day out, but there is no attempt to follow any of these through together, limited progress will also be made. Your team needs to be aware of the dangers of 'PLU' teams and the benefits of balanced approaches.

Dr Meredith Belbin has spent over 20 years researching the nature, structure and behaviour of teams, and his highly respected work on Team Role Theory provides a clear profile of the basic personality types you need to include in an effective team. If you want to know more about Belbin's work, team role analysis or team role workshops, you can contact Belbin Associates Limited at:

> 3–4 Bennell Court
> West Street
> Comberton
> Cambridge
> CB3 7DS
> Tel: (01223) 264975

Even if you have effectively balanced your team, you will often find they pass through different phases as they develop.

### Form

During the start-up phase of a new team, members tentatively explore the boundaries of acceptable group behaviour. As the team forms, they want to establish themselves as participants and worry about being left out.

### Storm

Team members realise that their job is difficult and grow impatient with lack of progress. They argue about the actions the team should take, rely on their personal and professional experience, resist collaboration and become irritable/stubborn.

### Norm

Team members reconcile competing loyalties and responsibilities. They recognise the importance of rules and appropriate behaviours. Competitive relationships become more collaborative and the team members begin to work with each other.

### Perform

Team members discover one anothers' strengths and weaknesses, understand and accept their roles and work in synergy towards meeting their objectives. (Adapted by Townsend and Donovan from B W Tuckman – see Further Reading).

## COMMUNICATION SKILLS

Communication skills can improve interpersonal relationships and collaboration within your team. If what they do is fairly simple, then being competent, polite and organised may well be enough. If your team are involved in more complex processes involving complicated decision-making, they will require more sophisticated listening, presenting and negotiation skills.

## OPTIONS AVAILABLE FOR TEAM BUILDING

Your team is the bridge between individual and organisation. By managing the performance of individuals only, you will miss out on all kinds of opportunities and miss a number of threats, too. Team building is a crucial part of maintaining a safe and effective team.

Traditional military team building puts members through shared and demanding experiences. Being pushed to extremes and having to struggle to survive establishes a bond among those who share the experience. This learning can be enhanced further when members have to co-operate and work together to get through it.

The principles of this type of team building are used to underpin Outward Bound and other outdoor activities/ residential weekends. However, there are many team builders who use gentler methods of helping members of the team get to know one another well.

### Developing a sense of belonging

The team builder's main priority is to develop a strong and positive sense of belonging. You can do this by creating conditions where the members of the team start perceiving themselves as 'us'. One of the major problems you might face if you work within a large organisation is the traditional structure, which might stand in your way. For example, if you task your team with developing a strategy to deal with complaints quickly and effectively, but the organisation demands that they adhere to bureaucratic systems already in place, your team members will become demoralised and much less enthusiastic about taking the time to make proposals in the future.

Nicky Hayes identified four different approaches to building a team, which can be identified in organisational literature:

- interpersonal
- role based
- values based
- task based.

## Interpersonal

Focuses on developing very high levels of social and personal awareness among team members. Team members must be carefully trained to listen. They need to be aware of one anothers' social situation and to develop more effective communication channels. This approach works on the premise that if team members understand one another well enough, they will work together effectively. There are a number of different ways you can do this, but the principle is that open and candid discussion about relationships and conflicts will generate a culture of trust and confidence.

## Role based

This approach emphasises role definition as a major task. The aim is to clarify each individual's role expectations and shared responsibilities of the different members. The most important part of this approach is that team members are allowed to see themselves 'from the outside'. This lets team members reflect on their own styles of interaction and teaches them how to change their style to help the team, as a whole and operate more effectively.

## Values based

Values based team-building focuses on developing a shared understanding between team members. This emphasis is on what really matters to them, i.e. their values. If you can make sure everyone in the team holds common values and that the working aims of the team reflect those values, members should be able to work together effectively. They will also be able to perceive how their own part contributes to the overall activity of the team. Team away-days can be particularly valuable, so that you can all focus on a shared vision.

## Task based

The emphasis on this approach is less about what people are like and more about what they can do. There is, therefore, a heavy emphasis on the exchange of information among team members. It also highlights a systematic approach to the task in terms of resources, skills and practical steps. A high performance team using this model learns to excel as a direct result of undertaking challenging tasks. As they deal with them, they learn new skills through tackling the problems and obstacles set.

Most team building activities use one of these four approaches, if not a mixture.

## MENTORING

Faced with anchoring highly mobile 20-somethings, many companies are exploring the idea of a mentoring programme as an inexpensive way to improve team building. An in-vogue subject since the 1970s, mentoring has traditionally meant a seasoned manager sharing insight and experience with a less experienced person, to further their career and tutor them on 'the way things are done'. However, the role of mentoring is changing from teacher/learner to knowledge exchange via peers and partners.

Running a mentor programme within your team ensures that all members have a point of contact and have access to feedback. Mentoring is a skill in itself and requires some preparation. If you can identify a mentor as soon as a new member has been recruited, they can start to establish a relationship with their trainees before they even meet. This relationship can be crucial to the success of individual team members and should be a prime focus. Mentors will need some briefing on their role, which should be underpinned by the following principles.

### Principles for mentoring

1. Keep the relationship on a professional level, particularly where there are differences in gender. Sensitivity to potential misinterpretation in language and behaviour will be important in these situations.

2. Understand the distinction between counselling and advising and wherever possible encourage the trainee to

work out their own solutions with you acting only as a sounding board.

3. Remember you will be a role model and that how you are seen to manage in day to day situations at work will affect the relationship you have with the trainee.

4. Feedback you give should be clear, honest and constructive and designed to build confidence and ongoing commitment in your colleague.

5. Be sensitive to age differences and the anxieties that people will experience when acquiring new skills.

6. When giving feedback, remember the three Cs. It should be **clear**, **constructive** and **confidence boosting**.

## EXERCISES

There are some excellent collections of team building activities, which are designed for use with teams of various sizes. It is worth investing in one of the following:

*Ready Made Activities for Developing your Staff*, David Taylor and Sue Bishop (Pitman Publishing: 1994 London).
*101 Games for Trainers*, Bob Pike and Christopher Busse (Lakewood Books: Minneapolis 1995).
*Games Trainers Play*, John Newstrom and Edward Scannell (McGraw-Hill: London 1980).
*Even More Games Trainers Play*, Edward Scannell and John Newstrom (McGraw-Hill: London 1994).

## SUMMARY

High-performance teams don't just happen, they must be built. Leading a group of people who just happen to occupy the same building on weekdays is not a matter of keeping an eye on what they do and intervening if things start to go wrong.

Most of us inherit a team and then bemoan the fact that they are not what we would have chosen. Investing some time and energy into looking at the people you work with, what matters to them, what skills, knowledge and attitudes they have and what they need, will benefit them, you and the organisation. Some effort will also need to be invested in building and maintaining your team.

A mentor system has revolutionised the way some organisations have run. By setting up a system and preparing team members to take on the roles of mentor and trainee, you can help to establish the kind of culture which encourages team members to stay with your organisation and flourish.

## ACTION POINTS

1. Talk to members of your team and explore whether they consider themselves to:
   a. have common goals and work together to achieve them
   b. have a clear identity as a special group
   c. interact positively with others in the organisation
   d. generate a positive and enthusiastic approach
   e. communicate clearly and effectively
   f. work together more effectively than each individual would.

2. If the answer to any of these questions is no, what measures can you take to improve the situation?

3. What team building/maintenance strategies do you plan to put in place for the next 12 months?

# Conclusion

The most important part of this book is to practise what you have learned, not just during training sessions, but as part of your day to day life. It is always tempting to skim over the action points at the end of each chapter. However, each point has been carefully included, not just as an extra task to fill in your time, but as a structured way of making sure that training for your team is a success. If you've missed some of them out, go back. Look at them again. If you complete them you'll find that they will actually save you time in the long run.

For those of you who have considered training to be a chore in the past, I hope you are filled with the energy and enthusiasm to do this part of your job justice. For those of you who haven't been involved in training before, I hope you will have the confidence to try ideas out and to take some risks. For those of you who already enjoy training and realise the importance of the investment, I hope you have picked up some new ideas and approaches.

> **'The great aim of education is not knowledge but action'**
> *Herbert Spencer*

**Remember: You lose what you don't use**

# About the Author

Having trained as an emergency nurse in the early 1980s, Lisa Hadfield-Law held a number of positions running emergency teams around the UK. During this time she focused on training teams of professionals how to respond to major incidents, including the Kings Cross fire and the Baltic Exchange bombing.

From 1989, Lisa worked with the Advanced Trauma Life Support Committee at the Royal College of Surgeons of England to establish training for doctors and nurses in the management of patients with major injuries. This training is now considered to be the 'gold standard' for trauma management in the UK.

In 1992, Lisa visited the US as a Smith and Nephew Scholar, to look at managing stress in high performance teams. For the last decade Lisa has been involved with helping groups in this country and abroad to lead and work with teams under pressure.

Lisa left the NHS in 1997 to widen her experience of training teams. Since then she has worked with: over 50 different primary care and hospital Trusts in the UK, US, Sweden and New Zealand; the Private Patient Managers Forum, Nuffield Hospitals; AO Maxillo Facial Surgeons – UK; Marks and Spencer Financial Services; Barclays Stockbrokers; Barings Asset Management; Fitzgerald & Law – accounting firm; Active Merchandising Company; Research Machines – IT software company and the armed forces.

Lisa has made over 1000 presentations at conferences and universities around the world over the last decade. She has published more than 50 articles and is the author of *Effective Presentations for Health Care Professionals*'.

Contact details:

Lisa Hadfield-Law
Baileys Consulting
Church Street
Charlbury
Oxfordshire
OX7 3PR

Tel: (01608) 811866
E-mail: lisahlaw@aol.com

# Further Reading

*Accelerated Learning for the 21st Century*, Rose, C & Nicholl, M J (Piatkus, London 1997).

*Active Talk – the effective use of discussion in learning*, Van Ments, M (Kogan Page, London 1990).

*Basic Training for Trainers*, Kroehnert, G (McGraw-Hill Book Company, London 1995).

*Dealing with Difficult Colleagues*, Wylie, P & Grothe, M (Piatkus, London 1993).

*Facilitation Skills*, Bee, F & Bee, R (Institute of Personnel and Development, London 1998).

*Getting What you Want*, Anderson, K (Penguin, London 1993).

*Handbook of Small Group Research* (2nd edn) Hare, A P (New York Free Press, New York 1976).

*How to Organise Effective Meetings and Conferences*, Seekings, D (Kogan Page Ltd, London 1996).

*How to Run Seminars and Workshops*, Jolles, R (John Wiley & Sons, New York 1993).

*Human Behaviour: an Inventory of Scientific Findings*, Berelson, B and Steiner, G (Harcourt Brace, New York 1964).

*I Can See You Naked*, Hoff, R (Andrews & McMeel, Kansas City 1992).

*No More Butterflies*, Desberg, P (New Harbinger Publications, California 1996).

*Non Verbal Communication*, Mehrabian, A (Aldine Atherton, Chicago 1972).

*Power Presentations*, Brody, M and Kent, S (John Wiley & Sons, New York 1993).

*Powerpoint 4 for Windows for Dummies*, Lowe, D (IDG Books, California 1994).

*Presentations for Health Care Professionals*, Hadfield-Law, L (Butterworth Heinemann, Oxford 1999).

*Successful Team Management*, Hayes, N (International Thomson Business Press, 1997).

*The Excellent Trainer*, Kamp, D (Gower, Hampshire 1996).

*The Facilitator's Pocketbook*, Townsend, J and Donovan, P (Management Pocket Book, Hampshire 1999).

*The Skilful Mind – an Introduction to Cognitive Psychology*, Gellatly, A (Open University Press, Milton Keynes, 1986).

*Training with a Beat*, Millbower, L (Stylus, London 2000).

*Training with NLP*, O'Connor, J and Seymour, J (Thorsons, London 1994).

*Troubleshooting for Trainers – Getting it Right when Things Go Wrong*, Seifert, L and Stacey, M (Gower, Hampshire 1998).

*Understanding Social Anxiety: Social Personality and Clinical Perspectives*, Leary, M (Sage Publications, California 1983).

*Winning Presentations*, Gilgrist, D and Davies, R (Gower, London 1996).

*Your voice can make or break you*, Driscoll, K (Rochester NY *Democrat and Chronicle*, 26 August 1993, p10b).

## WEB SITES

http://www.dale-carnegie.co.uk/teamdevelopment

http://www.microsoft.com/office/powerpoint/default.htm

http://www.theteamwork.co.uk

# Index